Breaking Through God's Silence

A Guide to Effective Prayer

David Yount

SIMON & SCHUSTER

SIMON & SCHUSTER
Rockefeller Center
1230 Avenue of the Americas
New York, NY 10020

SIMON & SCHUSTER and colophon are registered trademarks
of Simon & Schuster Inc.

Designed by Irving Perkins Associates

Manufactured in the United States of America

1 3 5 7 9 10 8 6 4 2

Library of Congress Cataloging-in-Publication Data
Yount, David.
Breaking through God's silence : a guide to effective prayer /
David Yount.
p. cm.
Includes bibliographical references and index.
1. Prayer—Christianity. I. Title.
BV210.2.Y68   1996
248.3'2—dc20   96-10660 CIP
ISBN 0-684-82419-1

Once again for
Rebecca

"And they called Rebekah, and said to her,
'Will you go with this man?'
She said, 'I will go.'"

—*Genesis 24:58*

This book is dedicated equally to every grown-up child who, having long since forgotten how to pray, has learned to love. As you will discover, they are one and the same thing.

Contents

Introduction: The Sound of Silence   11

1. How and Why We Pray   21
2. Breaking Through the Inner Barrier   27
3. The Voice at the Other End   48
4. Starting the Conversation   63
5. Cutting Through the Static   85
6. The Best Prayer and the Best Pray-er   104
7. A Brief History of Prayer   124
8. Prayer for Skeptics   149
9. Recipes from Prayerful People   165
10. Ten Keys to Effective Prayer   176
11. A Guided Treasury of Prayers   185

Author's Note   211
Index   215

Prayer

is the vital act by which the entire mind
seeks to save itself by clinging to the principle
from which it draws its life . . .
no vain exercise of words,
no mere repetition of certain sacred formulae,
but the very movement itself of the soul,
putting itself in a personal relation of contact
with the mysterious power of which it feels
the presence,—it may be even before it has a name
by which to call it.

—William James

Introduction
The Sound of Silence

"I am a voice shouting in the desert . . . "

John 1:23

On a cold bright day in October 1995, Harvard University scientists threw a switch that launched the Billion Channel Extra-Terrestrial survey. Now, round the clock, a radio telescope at Harvard's Agassiz Station observatory listens for a signal from space—even the faintest sign that suggests someone in the universe is listening to us. Within fifteen years a $300 million radio telescope three-quarters of a mile in diameter will be built somewhere on earth, extending our hearing 100 billion miles into space.

This vast and persistent effort at communication with the universe is neither the stuff of science fiction nor the quest of mad scientists. Northeastern University physicist Alan Cromer calls it "the space-age version of communicating with God," but adds that it is "garbled at best." To date, alas, there has been no response from the beyond.

The quest for a conversation with the universe is nothing new. The first man and woman on earth, finding themselves possessed of reason and curiosity, looked to the heavens in wonder for an answer to their predicament: Why am I here? What am I here for? What will become of me? In the more benign allegory in Genesis, Adam and Eve walked with God in

11

the Garden of Eden and conversed with him. Either way, from the outset of intelligent life on earth, mankind prayed.

A recent Gallup poll revealed that 90 percent of all Americans pray—75 percent every day. Since fewer than two-thirds of Americans belong to churches, prayer is clearly an activity that springs less from discipline than necessity. It is spontaneous rather than prescribed—perhaps instinctive for this creature called man. Most prayer is not communal (as in church), nor is it even spoken. It is mental—our unspoken message going out to the silence of God, by whatever name we address God. Prayer is as normal as breathing.

Given the prevalence of prayer, it is fair to ask how well we pray. Jesus' closest followers asked of him: "Teach us to pray." In response he gave them the words of what has come to be known as the Lord's Prayer, in which we address God as "our Father." When Christians worship in common, they follow formulas that age has rendered reliable. But when each of us prays alone, sharing our anguish and our aspirations, our guilt and our gratitude, we are on shiftier ground. From the time I was baptized, as an infant, until I was ordained, in my thirties, I prayed formally with others and memorized many prayers, but was never taught how to speak with God on my own. When I underwent a crisis of faith in my twenties, I no longer knew what to say.

I suspect your experience is not unlike mine. However articulate we are in everyday life, our personal prayers tend to be stilted or panicky or childish. It is true that there are no atheists in foxholes, but the quality of prayer in adversity is surely nothing to brag about. Grace under pressure is rare.

You do not have to be a Christian to pray—or a Jew or Moslem or, for that matter, a believer of any kind. Prayer is instinctive and spontaneous. Even the atheist cannot suppress the need to communicate what is in his heart. God goes by many names, and none. God is within and without—to be found equally in the cupboard of your own mind and heart and in the vastness of the universe. "What is beyond infinity?"

Einstein was once asked facetiously. "The face of God," he replied seriously. But one does not have to reach that far: God is also underneath your skin.

Whatever your religion (even if you are its own lonely God), on reflection you will agree that the purpose of life is to break through your solitude, to find self-knowledge and respect, to reach out to others and accept their love, and to communicate with your creator, who alone knows the blueprint from which you were made.

If you are not a Christian or are uncertain of your beliefs, do not be put off by the traditional religious orientation of these pages. It is your guarantee of reliability and a safeguard against eccentricity and trendiness. This is in essence a how-to book. Because prayer is not dogma but process, you can learn to pray effectively whatever your faith or skepticism. Just as Jesus was not himself a Christian (but a Jew), God is neither Christian nor Jew nor Moslem nor Buddhist nor Hindu but utterly ecumenical, and God is as much yours as he is mine. There is more than enough of God to go around; by definition, the Infinite is never in short supply.

"We do not know how to pray as we ought," Saint Paul affirms (Romans 8:26), but adds in the next breath that God's Spirit helps us to pray—indeed that the Spirit prays within us if we let him. You might imagine that if you were the Son of God you wouldn't be expected to pray (but only talk to yourself!), yet we know that Jesus prayed. The night before he was executed he took his closest companions with him and prayed that he might escape torture and death. Instead of joining Jesus in prayer, his fickle apostles fell asleep.

In contrast, God is always awake. Contrary to common belief, God is not silent at all. God hears and acts—not necessarily dispensing our prescriptions as we write them, but responding nonetheless. Prayer can be effective, but not as an exercise in wish fulfillment. As lovers, lottery winners, politicians, and entertainers attest, often the worst thing that can happen is to have one's prayers answered in one's own terms.

In the popular Garth Brooks song, the singer recalls his desperate prayer to have the love of a woman he now realizes would have been all wrong for him. Now happily married, he thanks God for unanswered prayers.

As we know, Jesus' own prayer that he be spared torture and death was not answered, but he knew his prayer was heard. He also knew he might be asking for the wrong thing, so he added: "But not as I will, but as you will." Breathing his last on the cross, Jesus offered prayers of reconciliation: "Father, forgive them, for they know not what they do," and finally, "Into your hands I commend my spirit."

If you believe—or wish to believe—that you are God's creature, made in God's image, with a destiny to live with God in happiness, then prayer is the natural expression of the relationship you have and will always have with God. If that is too much faith to swallow, but you acknowledge your solitude and need to reach out to your source (by whatever name), then you too are ready for prayer.

You and I cannot afford to be spiritually illiterate. It makes sense to learn to pray effectively. Among the benefits you will gain from prayer is the ability to focus your life, to expand your spirit, to rejoice in blessings and be calm in adversity, and to increase your faith and peace with your fellowmen. You will grow in integrity and in faith, hope, and love. Life will not necessarily become easier, but you will deal with it more easily and sensibly, and you will be a better person.

It will take some work. Personal prayer is not just the rote repetition of words; it is a regimen. Jesus and others gave us the right words to say when we speak to God, and his church has built a vast liturgy of common prayer that is completely reliable and can serve as the jumping-off point for our personal conversations with our creator. We need to learn what these formal prayers mean; then in the silence of our own hearts we will find our own voices and our own words. Like anything else that is worthwhile, prayer takes practice. In a sense it is like learning another language.

What I can assure you is that the lessons in the following pages are reliable, tested by two thousand years of Christian experience and almost as many years of Jewish tradition before that. In the 1960s it was fashionable to believe that consciousness-expanding drugs might prove to be shortcuts to God, delivering a pharmacological mysticism that would dispense with the discursive nature of traditional prayer and bring one face-to-face with God. The first person I ever knew who experimented with LSD was a theologian who taught in a seminary. He was all very innocent and well-intentioned, but his experience ended in a bad trip. He returned, shaken, to prayer.

None of the prescriptions for prayer in the following pages can be characterized as quick fixes, but they are reliable. And there are special aids to prayer that deserve a place in your life, because one or another may help you personally. I vividly recall a recent trip to San Francisco, where, in the shadow of Grace Cathedral, my wife and I watched Chinese men, women, and children patiently tracing the delicate maneuvers of tai chi, practicing their way to a peace that can only assist prayer. Moreover, meditation, biofeedback, hypnotism, martial arts, and exercise deserve to be included in any serious guide to effective prayer. By themselves these therapeutic activities are unrelated to religion, but they can help compose us in a prayerful state. We are none of us disembodied souls, yet we pray to a Spirit. Whatever helps us to focus is worth considering in our quest.

I have entitled these pages *Breaking Through God's Silence* because it is commonly thought that God does not speak. But the title is flawed. Every Jew, Christian, and Moslem knows that God speaks and acts. The Old and New Testaments and the Koran do not chronicle humankind's search for God but rather God's successful search to restore contact and make a covenant with his creatures. Although prayer feels like our reaching out to God, in fact it is our *response* to him: God has already embraced us; he holds the whole world (and you and me) in his hands.

Nevertheless, prayerful people (which is to say, most of us) complain of God's silence, especially when we call out in moments of need and desperation and hear only the echo of our own voices. While God is not really silent, neither is God a conversationalist. Like a doctor, God expects the patient (us) to do most of the talking. The better we can explain our symptoms, the easier it is for God to offer a diagnosis and prescribe a remedy.

The only occasion on which my own doctor is talkative is at the end of my annual physical. That's when he tells me things I don't want to hear—that I must exercise more, cut down on alcohol, fat, and cholesterol, and devote more time to my family than to my career. Through the Bible and his church (and our parents), God has been counseling us all our lives, but we don't like God's interference any more than the doctor's warning to change our habits. When things are going well we *welcome* God's silence. As we learn love, peace, and patience from God, we will at length find our voices and no longer need to complain when God keeps still.

You can learn to pray at your own pace. No one but you (and God) will know how well you are progressing. No tests will be administered and no grades will be given. But you will not be able to fake prayer any more successfully than you can fake marriage, parenting, or friendship. Either we are sincere or we are phony. Prayer above all is honesty with God.

That understood, nothing should deter you from getting started. Are you unsure of your faith—uncertain whether God even exists? Then pray for faith. You have lots of company in your uncertainty, including me. As a young man I found myself questioning God's existence, after a childhood of certainty. Although blessed in every other part of my life, I was miserable in my doubt. So much so that I did something that in retrospect seems melodramatic: I broke an engagement to be married, rejected fellowships to graduate school, entered a monastery and then a seminary, where I remained for eight years, most of them still in the agony of doubt. I thought at the time that I was searching to prove God's existence. In that quest I read theological tomes as tedious as telephone directories, trying to convince myself that there had to be a First Cause, a Prime Mover, an Infinite Perfection, an eternal Ground of Being. It took me years to realize that my quest was wrongheaded. What solace could there be in proving the existence of an abstract Prime Mover when what I really needed was a Father whose Son died for love of me? During those years, like a terrier with a shoe, I could not for the life of me let go of God, yet I pretended to doubt his existence. At length, exhausted and conscious of the vanity of my search, I realized that the only proof I would ever obtain had to come from God and that it would always coexist with doubt. To this day my proof of God's existence is that I cannot be indifferent to him.

Your experience will differ from mine. Nevertheless, faith remains a virtue because doubt plagues the believer as well as the skeptic. So pray for faith, but do not pray for goodness—at least not at the outset. Pray instead for forgiveness and for a better understanding of what it is about you that requires God's forgiveness as well as the forgiveness of those with whom you live and work. Because most of us are small-time sinners, we flatter ourselves that there is nothing much wrong with us—that we are only "imperfect." Admittedly, most sins are not capital crimes; they are the products of our indifference to others' needs. Sin for most of us consists of what we fail to do for others and neglect doing for ourselves. Unfortunately, when we pray to be "good," we have in mind a kind of righteousness and benevolence that comes only at an advanced stage of spiritual growth. So beware of righteousness. Better to heed Jesus' story of the Pharisee and the publican:

Two men went up into the temple to pray, one a Pharisee and the other a tax collector. The Pharisee stood and prayed thus with himself: "God, I thank thee that I am not like other men, extortioners, unjust, adulterers, or even like this tax collector. I fast twice a week, I give tithes of all that I get." The tax collector, standing far off, would not even lift up his eyes to heaven, but beat his breast, saying, "God, be merciful to me a sinner!" I tell you, this man went down to his house justified rather than the other; for every one who exalts himself will be humbled, but he who humbles himself will be exalted.

Luke 18:10–14

The basis of prayer is the acknowledgement of our dependence on God and of our sinfulness. If sin is not a word in your vocabulary, then ponder your shortcomings—your failings as well as your offenses, your lack of generosity and responsibility, and the way you ration your love and service. Even at our worst we are never unworthy of seeking God's attention and relying on his forgiveness. After all, it was God who established our worth in the first instance and who sustains us despite our faults.

In the following pages we will look at models and modes of prayer, communal as well as personal, then explore techniques for assuming a prayerful state of mind. We will analyze the Lord's Prayer to determine how God wants to be approached. And we will listen to some people who have literally made of their lives one unbroken prayer. In journalistic fashion I will seek answers to the core questions: the who, what, when, where, why, and how of speaking with God.

Because personal prayer is a solitary enterprise, it is prone to eccentricity. We are tempted to domesticate God in personal prayer—to bring him down to our level as a bosom buddy, a kind of mirror image of ourselves. This temptation needs to be resisted. God is not our comrade; he is our Father. We are made in God's image; God is not made in ours. Historically God has chosen to work with groups of people, notably with Israel and with his church, selecting individuals not on their own merits but to be servants of his family—the family of humankind. Although we develop a personal relationship with God, God does not take on a personality for you or me different than he does for anyone else in the world or in history. We change; God is consistent and cannot be manipulated. We do not possess God; God possesses you and me. Limited as we are in this life to seeing God "as in a glass, darkly," we have plenty of information that God has revealed about himself, so there is no justification for treating him as a stranger. Obviously, the more we know about God, the better we can pray to him.

A note on style: with the assistance of my copy editor I have made the text as gender-neutral as possible. God, afterall, is not a sexist. But occasionally I get stuck in syntax and must refer to *him*.

1
How and Why We Pray

Personal prayer is completely and conveniently portable. Ordinary Americans pray not only on waking and retiring, but while exercising, commuting, cooking, housecleaning, listening to music, working, going into labor, and making love. You can even pray on a bus:

> On a bus to St. Cloud, Minnesota,
> I thought I saw you there,
> With the snow falling down around you
> Like a silent prayer . . . *

No time and no occasion is inappropriate for prayer, except those moments when we are determined to be self-absorbed, self-pitying, or vindictive.

In everyday life, prayer is a valuable substitute for daydreaming. So much of our lives consists of routines we cannot escape but that engage only a fraction of our attention and interest, leaving plenty of room for God.

In the Christmas 1994 issue of *USA Today Weekend*, author Jim Castelli reported on the prayer practices of two dozen Americans from all walks of life and a variety of religious faiths. "What stands out," he wrote, "is the amazing similarity in the

---

21

way we pray and what happens to us when we pray . . . Prayer isn't a game or hobby; it's something that people turn to in order to get through the things that seem impossible to get through."

Most of our prayers are cries for help or expressions of simple thanks. Prayerful people are grateful even in the midst of tragedy. Victims of natural disasters seldom curse God; rather, they exclaim, "Thank God, it could have been worse." When the daughter of the Reverend Robert Schuller of California's Crystal Cathedral lost a leg in a motorcycle accident, the prayer he said was one of thanksgiving: "Thank you, God, that she's alive. Thank you, God, that she lost just one leg. Thank you, God, that her face wasn't smashed. Thank you that her brain wasn't injured. Thank you that they got her to the hospital."

Castelli reported that most Americans describe their prayers as conversations, contacts, or connections—"just talking to God even when they are not sure who or what is on the other side of the conversation." He quotes Jane Redmont, a Catholic, who says, "I think of prayer primarily as listening." Richard Foster, a Quaker, notes with Carole Mu'min, a Moslem, that the words used in prayer are not magical formulas. "God isn't hard of hearing," Foster says. Mu'min adds that "the essence of prayer is not just the words, but the actual connecting."

Many Americans are drawn to prayer in awe and reverence. A mountain range, the ocean, or a sunset prompts them to address their creator and sustainer. For some, prayer is emotional. Sandra Goodwin Clopine, a Pentecostal Christian, finds prayer so overwhelming that she prostrates herself before God. Carole Mu'min, the Moslem, compares prayer to an "electrical charge." When singer Dan Seals prays, his emotion is so great that the hairs stand up on his arms and his heart feels as if it will burst.

For most Americans, however, prayer is more often tedious and arid, requiring a kick start. Reform rabbi Larry Kushner, for example, forces himself to see life's blessings in a fresh light each day rather than take them for granted. Many Americans offer formal thanksgiving before meals, but when these prayers become truly thoughtful, Kushner says, "I all of a sudden realize, just for a second: 'Oh, my God, I didn't make this food. I don't know how this food got here.' I really am dumbfounded before the experience of my own sustenance, my own nourishment."

Although most Americans improvise their personal prayers, many of us start with a favorite we have memorized. Jews may start with one or more blessings that begin, "Praised are you, Lord our God, king of the universe . . . " Christians are comfortable with the Lord's Prayer, addressed to "our Father." Prayerful people pause often during the day just to take stock of what they see and possess, and say, "Thank you, God." High Star, a Native American medicine man, has a simple prescription: "The way I pray is to get up every morning and say, 'Hi, God. Give me a good day.'"

Americans are more divided on *why* they pray—on what they expect to get out of connecting with God. Catholic psychologist Sidney Callahan offers a traditional explanation. "Prayer always makes you feel wonderful," she claims, "because it makes you feel more alive, or more spirited, or more happy, or more energized, or more peaceful. It opens up the world to me." Buddhist priest Ronald Nakasone prays because "it breaks our self-centeredness, because we come to understand that we are a part of a greater reality."

Those who attempt prayer as an exercise in wish fulfillment seldom complain about God's silence, because they are not interested in conversation or a relationship with him. God's existence for them is a matter of utility as impersonal as the Home Shopping Network: choose what you like, pick up the phone, and order. God is expected to manage the shipping and handling.

Recognizing this danger of approaching God in prayer as a year-round Santa Claus, some Americans hesitate altogether to make any specific requests, asking only that God's will be done. Lutheran theologian Martin Marty insists that prayer holds no

magical power to insulate believers from misfortunes that be-
fall others. "That's an unbiblical game," he says. "It's superstition . . . Things just happen. It rains on the just and the unjust
alike. To me, theology and prayer are what we do with what just
happened, what interpretation we put on it, what attitudes we
have toward it."

Given that caveat, Americans still instinctively call on God
for assistance in matters trivial (I lost my keys) and great (I lost
my husband), expecting an answer, even if it does not completely satisfy them. God's apparent silence may mean "no" or
"not yet" or "try again," but it is no more unresponsive than a
parent's answer to a child in the same terms.

The answers to prayer are often intangible: the gift of patience in one's trials, the lessening of suffering, greater faith or
love or confidence or forgiveness—or the courage to break a
habit and start over. These are adult needs, and few who approach God sincerely in prayer complain of leaving empty-
handed. The head of the National Council of Churches, Joan
Brown Campbell, told Jim Castelli:

> I believe God never answers prayers in a direct way. Cause
> and effect are not immediate in prayer. But I look over my
> life and say my prayers have been answered. One of my
> prayers has always been that I have a meaningful life, a full
> life, that I might be given things to do that make a differ-
> ence . . . I can look back and see a way in which prayers
> have been answered, but not the way I would have de-
> signed it . . . I have a much better life for having been
> guided than if I had been able, every step of the way, to do
> what I thought was the right thing to do.

The point of prayer is not to change God's mind. There are
thoughtful theologians, however, who believe that prayer
somehow unleashes God to do for us what he intends for our
good but what he could not accomplish without our participation. In this way of thinking, God limits himself by the free-

dom he has instilled in his creatures, and God can assist us only when we align our freedom with his. If this is so, prayer *works* precisely because we become God's collaborators and we make sense of the expression "God helps those who help themselves." While prayer does not change God's mind, it changes ours. For this reason Jewish tradition subordinates personal prayer to congregational worship. The *Authorized Prayer Book of the United Hebrew Congregations of the Commonwealth* (1992 edition) argues that

> prayer is intended to *impress* rather than *express* oneself . . . Since prayer is primarily not a channel for emotional self-expression—of baring one's heart—but an instrument for the evocation of fundamental truths that are to stir our hearts . . . the corporate outpourings of a congregation are clearly more impressive than the private devotions of a lone worshipper.

By its emphasis on fixed prayers at fixed times (incorporating teachings as well as petitions), Judaism guards against "a false, indeed pagan, understanding of prayer as a means of pacifying and propitiating the deity and thus of earning its favors."

Historically, prayer developed from the primitive practice of sacrifice; but as the prophet Isaiah warned, God does not need our offerings: *we* need them. The Hebrew prayer book insists that, like sacrifice, "prayer, if offered for the wrong motives, is . . . unacceptable."

The English expression "to pray" implies petition, but the corresponding Hebrew *tephilah* literally means "to judge oneself." Accordingly, the prayer book argues,

> the harder I pray, the more convinced I become that only God can help me, and that I need his help. Prayer thereby turns me into a better and more deserving human being:

in respect of all the favors for which I ask, I realize more and more my dependence on God and my own helplessness.

The Christian church derives the same cautionary theme from its Jewish foundation, agreeing that personal prayer easily degenerates into self-serving eccentricity. No man is an island; the one God is God of all, so we need to pray together and for one another. After all, the ultimate purpose of prayer is to reestablish the intimacy between creature and creator that was our original condition in Paradise. Despite humankind's countless and various petitions over a lifetime, there is but one ultimate object of prayer for everyone—to be joined with God for eternity.

Although prayer may be instinctive, instinct is no assurance of quality or effectiveness. If we are serious about prayer, the first step we need to take is inward, not outward—not to reach out to locate and grasp God, but to search inside and define ourselves. God knows who he is: God is the supreme realist. But you and I are less well defined and prone to self-deception, posturing, and the deadliest sin of all, indifference. Let us therefore begin to break through God's silence with an effort to see ourselves as God sees us:

Speak, Lord, your servant is listening.

1 Samuel 3:10

2

Breaking Through the Inner Barrier

᷎

"The reason angels can fly is because they take themselves so lightly."

G. K. Chesterton

Several times a year I am present when the president of the United States subjects himself to dining with the Washington press corps—social evenings that can only be characterized as supping with the sharks. The tradition of dining with one's critics goes back a century, however, and any newcomer to the White House would be considered a bad sport if he refused the invitation.

Since chief executives on these occasions are expected not only to acknowledge but to entertain the press, each president develops the fine art of self-deprecation to disarm the media. Ronald Reagan, no darling of the press, was peerless in this department. I cannot imagine the queen of England or the pope reverting to such hilarious self-effacement, but the American ritual of the roast reassures citizens that this is truly a democracy, in which the president takes his licks like the rest of us. Humor clears the air by addressing the human condition and provoking laughter in all of us, whereas vanity causes us to lose perspective. During his evenings with the Fourth Estate, the president, being the butt of his own humor, is acknowledging that he is, after all, despite the loftiness of the role we have afforded him with our votes, only human. Thus the Scot Geddes MacGregor prays:

> Lord, hold my hand, I'm tired of
> stumbling in dark alleys.
> Put me in the palm of your hand.
> Lord, lift me up.
> Show me that love is still around.

Only Human

Although we are inclined to count our humanness as vulnerability, in prayer it can be a source of strength. The roles we play in life, however responsibly, disguise the persons we are beneath our posturings—cloaking us even from ourselves. God formed us in our natures and characters, but God did not create the roles we play in life. Even if our scripts were thrust upon us by circumstances or by others, we come to define and value ourselves by our parts in life's drama—parent, breadwinner, patriot, householder, caretaker, lover, companion. Navigating through adolescence is tempestuous not only because of our raging hormones, but because we are quite literally attempting to find ourselves.

Normally, by the time we reach early adulthood, we have fashioned characters for ourselves by assuming roles. But make no mistake. We have not really found *ourselves;* rather, we have created a more or less fragile persona for ourselves based on what we do and how people relate to us. This ego manufacturing is nowhere more apparent than in the nation's capital, where I work. At even the most casual social event in Washington, strangers introduce themselves by their job titles, demanding in turn: "What do you do?" The clear implication is that, whatever you do to put bread on your table, you *are* your occupation.

This is not the question our maker puts to us. Possessing the only set of blueprints, God knows us better than anyone else (including ourselves), so our success in prayer depends on communicating with him authentically: as the persons he created us to be, not the characters we have created for ourselves. Ironically, the fundamental mystery in prayer is not "Who is God?" but "Who am I?" The quest for God through prayer is an adventure in stepping out of our assumed roles to communicate with God now and prepare for the time when we confront God face-to-face for eternity.

To give an example: parents are prone to lose a sense of themselves when their grown children have left the nest. After years of acting responsibly with our three daughters, my wife and I are now challenged with reinventing our marriage in midlife and reevaluating ourselves after our demanding, highly personal roles as hands-on parents disappear. The end of our role as supporters during our daughters' dependency will enable my wife and me to recreate our relationship, meanwhile reintroducing ourselves to our children, now independent adults, forging new relationships with each of them as friends and peers.

Rest assured, the shedding of assumed roles is not a trendy appeal for you to release your inner child (whatever that may be), but rather to assert your intelligent and unbiased adulthood. Saint Paul sets us straight:

> When I was a little child I talked and felt and thought like a little child. Now that I am a man my childish speech and feeling and thought have no further significance for me. At present we are men looking at puzzling reflections in a mirror. The time will come when we shall see reality whole and face to face! At present all I know is a little fraction of the truth, but the time will come when I shall know it as fully as God knows me!
>
> *1 Corinthians 13:11–12*

We pray because God instructed us to, and because we do not want to wait for eternity to speak with him. God has already broken through to reveal himself to mankind in history, in scripture and in the church. It remains for us to remove the barriers in us that prevent him from breaking through to us:

> Lord, give us weak eyes for things
> which are of no account,
> and clear eyes for all your truth.
>
> *Søren Kierkegaard*

Pretense and Reality

In Shakespeare's vision, all the world's a stage—a helpful orientation to prayer. In everyday life we are actors attempting to perform our parts with only an imperfect sense of the script or the ending. Yet we are determined to please the authors who write our script and judge our performance. Normally these are our parents, teachers, supervisors, and peers—our drama critics.

This is not a bad way to conceive of the human situation. It is certainly sounder than presuming that my limited personal experience, thoughts, and emotions constitute the real world—when they are only a tiny sliver of reality (and that viewed with the extreme prejudice of my ego). Viewed from this perspective, not one of us is *normal*, because we do not share the same experience; each of us, perforce, is an eccentric.

Reflect that an accomplished actor grasps fully the character he is playing, but the character does not know the actor. Sir Laurence Olivier knew Hamlet well enough to slip into his skin and psyche, but Hamlet never even heard of Olivier. Just so, we lose our real selves in the roles we play and find it increasingly difficult to leave the stage, shed our costume, and take off our makeup. "Come off it!" we demand of people who put on airs, and this is precisely what we must demand of ourselves when we confront our creator—the ultimate play-wright—now in prayer and later in eternity.

Shall I shed my false self and revert to the actor underneath, or shall I continue to take comfort in following what I think to be my script (because I am its partial author), thereby eluding my maker? Most assuredly I cannot face God as I face life: *self-defined* as black or white, man or woman, single or married, childless or parent, Republican or Democrat, slim or over-weight, skeptical or believing, cool or committed, liberal or conservative, white collar or blue, redneck or blueblood. From God's point of view I am none of these things. I am simply God's child grown to adulthood and called by him to him.

The things you pray *for* will be conditioned by your place in life and the responsible parts you play, but those roles will all end in eternity, and what is left will be God and you. So we would be well advised to preface all our prayers (in C. S. Lewis's words): "May it be the real I who prays; may it be the real Thou I speak to."

The Real Thou

Contrary to expectations, the hardest half of the prayer equation is learning to be authentic ourselves. Courting God is not an exercise in seduction but in humility. Because we assume God is silent, it is tempting to conclude that prayer is totally our initiative. In fact, God from the outset has assumed the initiative in communicating with us and our forebears. All of scripture gives testimony to God's breaking into history and making covenants (two-way connections) with his creatures. When you and I are inclined to complain about God's silence, we are really only referring to our disappointment that God has not sent us a *personal* message lately.

I confess that I have not been favored with the emotional conversion experience of many believers, but the lack of thundering enlightenment has not compromised my faith, nor should it lessen yours. We have a lot of company among the millions of faithful who were raised in faith from childhood and learned about God from what he told everyone about himself—which is a lot. The "real Thou" is a God who chooses to deal corporately with his creatures, playing no favorites. God is utterly democratic, but he is not thereby impersonal. One of God's advantages over us is to be simultaneously totally absorbed in every one of his creatures—living, dead, and to come—and totally attentive to you and me at this very moment. God is outside of time but enters it at will, most notably when he sent his Son to become one of us.

It is tempting to domesticate God—to give God human features and motives, thereby making him more accessible. This is no special compliment to him. We are made in *God's* image; God is not made in ours. However, Christians believe that God radically anthropomorphized himself once and for all when he gave us Jesus, who was both God and man. Acknowledging this, Christians are still tempted to tame their creator by fudging important distinctions. Clearly God cannot be "reduced" to Jesus, who prayed to his Father and obeyed him, and instructed us to do the same.

Over a period of two millennia, Christians in their prayers have been tempted to sidestep their true object—God—in favor of conversations with Jesus or his mother or the saints or loved ones now gone. There is nothing wrong with these side conversations as long as we admit that they are, ultimately, evasions. In prayer we must be prepared to confront God head-on:

> Grant us ears to hear,
> Eyes to see,
> Wills to obey,
> Hearts to love;
> Then declare what you will,
> Reveal what you will,
> Command what you will,
> Demand what you will.
>
> *Christina Rossetti*

Words Versus Music

C. S. Lewis, a convert to faith, for many years avoided any ready-made prayers except for the Lord's Prayer. He tells us that he attempted to pray using no words at all. When the Oxford don prayed for others, for example, he aimed at visualizing them rather than using their names. Late in life he still maintained that wordless prayer was probably superior "if one can really achieve it," but conceded that such prayer required a rare spiritual athleticism to be successful and was more likely to degenerate into make-believe or fabricated emotion. Lewis agreed with the French philosopher Pascal that his error in striving to pray without words was in flattering himself that he could accomplish every time what he knew he could do only sometimes. In prayer, as in much of life, we need alternative and backup systems. Ironically, the best is often the enemy of the good, and we cannot always be at our best. In prayer we must hunker down for the long haul, because what we do now will be our principal occupation in eternity.

God does not require words in any case, because he reads our hearts. But unless we articulate ourselves *to ourselves* we cannot carry on an intelligent conversation with anyone but will only babble unprocessed feelings. It may be helpful to you to conceive of prayer as music: communicating often without words, always moving, addressing the emotions as well as the intellect—ultimately indefinable in words. The words of your prayer only support the melody. In a song it is the melody we remember most, not the words. In your prayer you are establishing a theme that God will recognize, to which you will fit your words like lyrics.

Others have accomplished this before us, so do not be quick to dismiss prayers preserved from past times. The best of them express universal sentiments and, like music, can convert us from listeners to performers. In effect, we tap our feet and sing along with the saints as we repeat their prayers. Few of us are poets, nor is our prose always literate. Few great singers are as adept as composers. Rather than expend our energy and attention on composing special prayers for God, we are wise, at least at the outset, to use those of others. The saints did not copyright their sentiments. I have compiled a treasury of prayers as the last chapter of this book.

At the same time as we respect others' prayers, there is no intrinsic merit in simply aping their devotions. That would amount to mere performance, not personal prayer. As King Solomon affirmed, only you and I are familiar with "the plague of our own hearts," so it is good to speak from our own predicaments, rather than rely exclusively on off-the-rack formulas.

There are books that purport to instruct us, by examples, how to write business letters and even love letters. They may help at the outset, but ultimately is is *your* business with God and *your* love for him that you want to express in prayer. Cyrano learned eventually to speak for his own love, not another's; so must we. In any case, God does not want to be read to but to be talked to:

Here is my heart, O God;
Here it is with all its secrets.

Saint Augustine

Praying for and with Others

Keeping your personal prayers close to tradition offers the advantage of helping you avoid the inclination to invent your own personal religion. There is a dignity and ceremony to the prayers of the church, temple, and mosque that reflect your relationship to God and support reverence without diluting intimacy.

It is good to bring others into our prayers, both to join us and possibly to profit from them. We are never alone in our prayers. Scripture tells us that the saints and angels and all the company of heaven are forever praying. Prayer is the lingua franca of heaven. The vast majority of our fellow citizens in every walk of life pray daily. Monks pray every possible hour. Like radio waves in the ether, prayer abounds but never becomes confused, because God hears on every frequency.

We pray with our bodies as well as our spirits. Just as we dress our bodies to suit life's occasions, we use them in prayer to express our attitude. Soldiers stand at attention. In Christianity the tradition of standing for prayer is ancient; kneeling is more recent. At one time monks prayed with arms outstretched, denoting both their openness to God and the posture of Jesus on the cross. Palms joined in prayer direct our prayers to God and reflect our dependency. In the earliest centuries of Christianity (as still in Judaism), it was the practice to pray aloud even when alone, to show that the whole creature (not just a disembodied spirit) is attending to God. Assemblies of believers pray and sing together, not least to demonstrate their solidarity and mutual need under the same creator and sustainer.

These are only techniques (not surefire solutions), but worth a try. Often when I do not know what to say or have no more than an instant to pray, I touch the cross on my bedroom wall or the one on a chain around my neck next to my skin. In that gesture I try to convey volumes. Remember that you will enter eternity bodily in a new creation, so pray with both body and spirit. Sometimes when you have no words and no emotions you may choose just to kneel silently or hold your hands in a prayerful attitude. You are simply attending to God. God is not keeping score.

As you begin to pray more often, you will encounter distractions, but absolute silence is not always necessary. Sometimes the white noise of city life or an air conditioner can blot out particular distractions and serve as a background to prayer. During protracted bouts with insomnia earlier in my life, I found that the recorded sound of ocean breakers and a lulling voice cleared my mind and helped me rest. We can learn to concentrate without great effort in any number of circumstances, even the one I was in as I wrote these lines—in a dentist's chair waiting for novocaine to numb my jaw! We can pray anywhere and anytime.

Paying Attention

It is God's attention to us that keeps us in existence. In that respect God is always paying attention to us, even when we do not think about him. When we focus attention, nothing happens in God; the *only* change is in us. What was formerly passive (or latent or forgotten) becomes active. Instead of merely being known, we begin to show and tell. In prayer we offer ourselves to view, in effect proclaiming, "Here I am."

Since God is always paying attention to us, our prayer is never presumptuous—only complementary. Communicating with God is like listening to the radio: there is always something to hear, but we must turn it on. In a radical sense, it is only by God's initiative that we can open a conversation: "For it is by the Holy Spirit that we cry 'Father.'" Christians believe that by opening ourselves to grace, we free God's Spirit in us to pray for us: not just human to God but God to God!

What shall we speak to God about? The four traditional themes of prayer are praise, sorrow, gratitude, and petition, with petition bringing up the rear because it smacks of selfishness. In reality, asking God for things we need is fundamental to prayer and nurtures the habit of humility. By going to God in small matters we gain the courage to approach him in big ones. "We must not be too high-minded," C. S. Lewis warns, or "deterred from small prayers by a sense of our own dignity rather than God's. God is in some measure to a man what that man is to God. The door in God that opens is the one I knock at." Of course, God knows best what we need, but it is slothful to leave the initiative to him. We must knock at the door, and often.

Nor must we allow guilt to stand in our way. We are all at fault—so much so that Christians contend that God had to send his Son to die for our guilt. But our redemption is accomplished. We know from experience that true guilt and guilt *feelings* are not necessarily related. Many hardened criminals feel no shame at all, whereas others of us are quick to blame ourselves for the slightest trespass. Wallowing in guilt is an affront to our creator and the length God has gone to save us from ourselves. We must therefore begin our prayers in confidence. When Jesus called for our conversion, he was not asking us to dwell on our shortcomings but literally to "turn around" from self to God. Every time we pray we are turning around:

> Almighty . . .
> Forgive
> My doubt,
> My anger,
> My pride.
> By thy mercy
> Abase me,
> By thy strictness
> Raise me up.
>
> *Dag Hammarskjöld*

Asking and Answering

While we must ask for things in prayer, we must not necessarily expect to get them. Christians note that Jesus' fervent prayer to be spared torture and execution was answered with a "no." If God can turn down his own Son, we should not be too easily put off. It is clear that some prayers are not answered because we are not ready for their fulfillment or because we are asking for the wrong things. Bernard Shaw and Oscar Wilde (neither of them great believers) warned that often the greatest curse is to get what we think we want. Fairy tales are full of plots in which the hero gets three wishes that, once granted, turn out to be curses.

This is more than fairy-tale reality. Many political economists, for example, believe we live in a zero-sum society, in which nothing good happens to one sector without depriving another. In certain obvious respects, our prayer seeks to gain personal advantage in a zero-sum world. The farmer whose prayer for rain is answered deprives the vacationer of a sunny holiday. The team whose prayer to win is satisfied ensures that its opponents will be losers. During great wars, whole nations pray aloud for victory, yet all enemies cannot prevail. For every winner there is a loser. By this reckoning, every time we pray for something for ourselves, we are implicitly acknowledging that, like Robin Hood, we are stealing from someone else.

This explains why some prayers are not answered, and it also suggests better objects of prayer. If all nations prayed for peace instead of victory, for example, no one would suffer. If we prayed for prosperity and then worked to increase it every-where, everyone would win and no one would lose.

So it is wise to approach God in the same spirit we would ap-proach a friend for a loan or a supervisor for an advance on salary. Our request is not peremptory, but couched in polite conditions: "Please, if it's convenient," or, "If you won't miss it." This is akin to praying with Jesus: "not as I will but as you will." Nevertheless, we must not be so polite with God or so certain that our wishes will meet with his disfavor that we fail to ask God for what we think we need. Above all, we must be honest with God, for that ensures that we will be honest with our-selves. If we are misguided in our desires, God will guide us—if we let him.

We should be cautious about asking God for self-knowledge, which, although it may be the beginning of wisdom, is some-thing we can tolerate only in small doses. Psychiatrists, after all, refrain from telling their patients what they really think of them; rather, they let patients talk out their troubles in the hope that directed self-discovery will lead to improvement. Be-ware of asking even your closest friend, "What do you really think of me?" The answer could be devastating. So too with God. In prayer we may often ramble like a psychiatric patient on a couch, and God (were he less than divine) would have every right to be bored to tears. Fortunately, God is infinitely patient and loving and interested. But make no mistake: God is no flatterer. Humility is always the sensible approach to him:

> O Savior . . .
> Annihilate the selfhood in me,
> Be thou all my life.
>
> *William Blake*

Do We Change God's Mind?

Isn't prayer a plea for God to change his mind—to do something he never intended until we asked? It certainly seems that way. How then are we to reconcile our requests of God with his changelessness?

Without stepping on the toes of theologians, the simplest answer is that the eternal mind does not change; rather, our prayers have eternally been taken into account. All this means is that there is no "before" and "after" for God (although there is for us). Prayer makes a difference—but an eternal one. To safeguard God's eternal changelessness, some theologians have claimed that the divine hands are tied: that everything that will ever happen is *predestined*. If that were true, prayer would be a sham and the great religious leaders would be misleading us by telling us to pray. In reality, predestination does not tie God's hands, because there is no "pre" in God. God is not limited by time. Our prayers, although pronounced in our time, figure into God's eternal will. Our prayers are heard not only before we pray but before we were created.

(If this kind of philosophical problem doesn't bother you, so much the better. But if argumentative people disturb your prayers, you have an answer for them.)

To my mind the knottier question is whether God is somehow limited in what he can do for us. We look at all the misery in the world and ask: why doesn't a good God do something about it? I spent some time in my book *Growing in Faith* addressing this problem, which mystifies us all and could conceivably deter you from praying. It's worth a brief reprise.

There is no completely satisfying explanation to the problem of a good God who is powerful and sovereign over a world that tolerates tragedy. Pain remains a paradox to even the most knowledgeable believers; still, it is not an utter mystery. The Bible is filled with stories about the trials of men and women whom God chose for his missions. God did not spare his friends, nor did God spare his Son from torture and death. They had missions.

But that still does not explain why the innocent suffer. It is one thing to choose heroism, quite another to be an unwitting victim. To unravel this mystery we should note two things: (1) much that goes wrong in life is accidental, not intentional, and (2) much that accounts for pain is caused not by God but by people, to themselves and to one another. Can we blame God for the excesses of nature that engulf men, women, and children in their turmoil? Not unless we expect that God sits in a control room twenty-four hours a day pressing all of nature's buttons.

And can we blame God for the murders, rapes, and wars caused by human beings? Again, unless God were to brainwash us and control us like robots, our freedom and our perversity will always allow us to commit outrageous acts of injustice, oppression, and selfishness against our fellow men and women.

We are left with a mystery, but one in which men and women are responsible for taming the dumb excesses of physical nature and their own natures. Accordingly, we do not expect miracles every time we pray, but we do expect God to listen and to care, and God does. This in many cases is the only immediate answer to our prayers. We need most of all to be listened to, not to be ignored. Beyond that we can survive disappointment. God, after all, is not Santa Claus.

The Unpredictable

We pray in part because we cannot predict with confidence. In the final analysis, the universe may be like a finely constructed clock. But even scientists do not understand all its workings, and in everyday experience the exceptions seem as frequent as the rules—the eccentricities as dramatic as the regularities. We do not pray for the sun to rise tomorrow; we know it will. But even meteorologists have been known to pray for rain, because their predictive power in the face of something as complex as the weather is limited. All we know with certainty is the consequences of general laws, not particularities.

The poet William Blake in any case warned that "to generalize is to be an idiot." Everything important to me—my wife, children, friends, work, home, health, and faith—is particular, not general, and therefore vulnerable. So I pray for them and for myself. And we pray in common for what is more momentous—victory in a battle, recovery from an operation, reciprocity in love. The world is full of Monday-morning quarterbacks who pretend to know why something was inevitable. They could better profit from their prescience by betting on horse races. The rest of us must do the best we can in the face of uncertainty, and then pray over it.

A final thought: if we could predict *every*thing, it would not necessarily alter *any*thing. Only the most morbid Christians would want to know when and how they will die, or even when next they will be seriously ill. Better to pray for a long and healthy life. What makes Jesus' prayer in Gethsemane so poignant and agonized is that he momentarily lost the certainty of his torture and death. He had been predicting it all along and had steeled himself to it. But now, like a prisoner on death row, he sensed the faintest possibility of a reprieve. Jesus was at that moment most like the rest of humankind, suffering in his uncertainty and praying to be spared.

It is worth noting that in Jesus' anguish he turned everywhere for aid and was denied it by *everyone:* by God (whose will was otherwise), by his apostles (who slept through his tortured prayer, then deserted him), by his church (Peter, who denied he even knew Jesus), by the government (Pilate, who washed his hands of him), and by the people (who chose to release Barabbas in his stead). Jesus knew all about unanswered prayers but was undeterred in his mission.

Moving Mountains

How can we reconcile unanswered prayers with the promises that faith will move mountains? Discounting the Semitic hyperbole (who has a serious need to have mountains moved anyway?), we are still confronted with consistent reassurances that our prayers will be answered. I suspect the solution lies in the quality of faith we bring to our prayers and the extent to which we attach conditions to our requests (for example, "I want this woman to marry me and to give me her answer no later than Saturday"). The faith that moves mountains is clearly not faith in mountain moving but faith in God, and it does not carry an expiration date. People have been praying for the collapse of communism as well as for racial freedom in South Africa for decades. Because the desired results took so long in coming, it is tempting to conclude that they happened without benefit of prayer. That is an unwarranted conclusion.

The faith that moves mountains is the kind of faith that allows us to pray not simply for a personal favor but as God's collaborator, actively seeking to ensure that God's will be done. Such prayer is a conscious contribution to a course of events that is created like a work of art in which each contributor is both an end and a means. In Christian terms, the faith that moves mountains is a massive collaboration to confirm the kingdom of God on earth. It is the faith that seeks justice and peace, equity and the reign of love for all—not just everyday personal needs.

By way of example, here from *The Book of Common Prayer*

(1980) is the church's prayer for a stillborn baby or a child who has died in infancy:

Heavenly Father, whose Son our Savior took little children
into his arms and blessed them;
Receive, we pray, your child into your never-failing care and
love,
Comfort all who have loved (it) on earth,
And bring us all to your everlasting kingdom.

Praying for Others

We find it easier to pray for others than for ourselves, largely because we minimize, or at least oversimplify, their needs (whereas we tend to exaggerate our own). Lord, find my daughter a husband! Get my son a job! Cure my wife's back pain! These are worthy prayers for others but probably mirror neither the extent nor the priority of the things for which they pray themselves. While it is easier to pray for others than for ourselves, it is often harder to *do* things for others than for ourselves. Once we start praying, it will become clear that we need to take an active helping role.

In the traditional Protestant view, it is useless to pray for the dead because their eternal status has already been decided for them. They have sealed their fate in this life; God has done all he can for them. The flaw in this line of thought is the same as in a simplistic notion of predestination. Although we live, die, and pray in time, God is not limited by our "before" and "after." He figures everything into the scheme of things eternally. My prayer today for my parents who died years ago is anticipated eternally by God. No matter that it is uttered after their death; the prayer counts eternally where they are now—outside of time.

You do not have to believe in a Dantesque purgatory to be doubtful whether all the dead feel themselves prepared to meet God and live with him eternally. At life's end, many of us may in all honesty admit we are ill prepared for eternity and enroll *voluntarily* in some heavenly version of finishing school to have our rough edges taken off. If my fancy is correct, then the people we love who have died have all the more need for our prayers.

Getting Started

Anything worth doing is worth doing badly, G. K. Chesterton counseled, reflecting that the alternative is usually to do nothing at all. Compulsive golfers and gamblers exemplify this wisdom, and it can serve us also as we begin earnestly but awkwardly to pray often. The critical thing is to acknowledge that prayer is work worth doing, despite our reluctance to bare ourselves to God. Effective prayer requires the humility to attempt it knowing we will be clumsy. As a child I was given prayers to say as a penance, that is, as a *punishment,* not unlike being compelled in school to write the same sentence over and over again on the blackboard. Often prayer is not especially pleasant, but then neither is physical training or cramming for an exam. The distinction is that we exercise and study to gain a payoff, whereas we pray even though our request may be deferred, modified, or even denied.

We pray because it is the most authentic thing we can do this side of the grave, just as it is the authentic activity in eternity. The universe is charged with the presence of God, and God alone is our destiny. Like art, prayer has an immediate objective (attention) and an ultimate goal (transcendence). By selection and concentration the artist in effect says: Look at this. Don't be distracted. Pay attention. (After Andy Warhol, can we ever take a soup can for granted?) The effective artist, by concentrating on the particular, enables us to transcend it and glimpse a corner of eternity.

As you begin to pray in earnest, reflect that the world is always crowded with God, so you don't have to make a trip, even a mental one, but just stay where you are. Nor need you be formal. Disraeli accused his nemesis, Gladstone, of treating Queen Victoria "like a public department." The object of your prayer is not an institution; God is personal.

Beware of drifting into daydreams or prescinding from the particular. The particular is what is real for us, and prayer is based on reality. Pay attention to the concrete: here I am in this place and my particular predicament, with these hopes and fears—not dreaming, not hallucinating, not escaping my uniqueness, but instead acknowledging God's presence in it. Begin by asking God to tell you who you are and what you need, to reawaken you to your real situation, your prospects and your obligations. Ask him to open you up, to strip you of pretense. If you know where you are, if your feet are planted on the ground and you are open, he cannot help but find you. Articulating your needs will help you get in touch with yourself. Knock on the door and it will be opened, but choose the door carefully. Don't wander all over God's neighborhood knocking on doors, but concentrate. In prayer, as in much that matters, more is not necessarily better.

Because you will find devotion awkward at the outset, start by familiarizing yourself with existing prayers. At the end of this book I have gathered many good ones; they reflect universal needs and sentiments, so you can appropriate them, alter them, and make them your own. The more you know about others' devotions, the more you will build your own prayer vocabulary and find fluency. When you are tongue-tied in prayer, that is the time to borrow another's prayer or just be silent and let God speak in his silence.

The Lord's Prayer is in many respects the perfect prayer, whether you are a believer or a skeptic. It covers all the bases— praise, penitence, gratitude, and petition. I've devoted a whole chapter in this book to that one brief prayer, and others to techniques for effective meditation. However, learning to pray effectively is not like perfecting your golf swing or your approach to the opposite sex. Technique alone will not get you far. You are not investing in God in the manner of a speculator on the stock market. Rather, you are seeking to open yourself to him, which calls more for passivity than for activity. As the psalmist counseled, "Be still, and know that I am God."

Devotion and Emotion

Do not mistake emotion for devotion. Most times you will pray and feel little or nothing. Religion is not unlike a good marriage after the honeymoon. Our best prayers are least supported by feeling but are acts of will aided by long habit.

You will start by going after God as if he were an object—a divine *something*. But as you progress, you will find that God is more elusive and richer—qualitative, more like light and music than substance. When you do find God, do not be grasping. As you discover something that works in your prayer, treat it as the poet Blake approached joy: by kissing it as it flies. We do not possess God in any case; God possesses us.

As you progress and require fewer words in your prayers, you will begin to favor mental images over mere words. It is wise not to attempt to control them unless they are only distractions. Instead, let God speak to you in his elusive, mysterious way. At its best your prayer will rise and burst like bubbles in champagne. Any attempt to capture effervescence is doomed to failure. The bubbles will escape and the champagne will go flat. Do not try to control the conversation; otherwise it will go flat.

Finally, find God in pleasures. There are many more innocent pleasures in our lives than we take the time to attend to. Perversely, we concentrate on many things that please us not at all. Find God in pleasures small and large. A sunny day or a smiling face is an occasion for thanksgiving. Treat all that pleases you as an invitation to speak to the one with whom you will spend an eternity of joy.

What will that be like? Here is C. S. Lewis's surmise as a Christian:

> Then the new earth and sky, the same yet not the same as these, will rise in us as we have risen in Christ. And once again after who knows what eons of the silence and the dark, the birds will sing and the waters flow, and lights and shadows move across the hills, and the faces of our friends laugh upon us with amazed recognition.

"Guesses, of course, only guesses," Lewis confessed. "If they are not true, something better will be. For 'we know that we shall be made like him, for we shall see him as he is.'"

God may often seem silent, but we do not pray to a mystery. The creator does not hide his hand. His revelation of himself has given us every cause to love him, to anticipate eternity with him, and to motivate our prayer now. An anonymous Mexican prayer expresses both humility and promise:

> I am only a spark
> Make me a fire.
> I am only a string
> Make me a lyre.
> I am only a drop
> Make me a fountain.
> I am only an anthill
> Make me a mountain.
> I am only a feather
> Make me a wing.
> I am only a rag
> Make me a king.

3

The Voice at the Other End

I have already noted the fervent efforts of tax-supported researchers to beam messages into outer space in the hope that, one day, they will be acknowledged and answered. In his novel *Contact,* atronomer Carl Sagan has speculated about what might transpire if the scientists' prayers are answered. And he cautions that the response of aliens may not be altogether reassuring to us earthlings.

God Spoke First

In these pages we will set ourselves a similar task—to break through God's silence through prayer. But unlike the silence of space, God's silence is only apparent, not real; and unlike the prospect of aliens, God's presence is thoroughly reassuring. Before man and woman even thought to pray, God spoke, and God has continued to reveal himself through the ages. We do not have to coax a response from our maker; he put in the call to us. No matter that we pretend that prayer is our initiative; it is always our response to God's call. We choose or refuse to pick up the receiver; the voice is always there at the other end.

Years ago, after a spate of obscene phone calls, my wife and daughters decided to install an answering machine in our home carrying a bare-bones message in my voice. The ploy worked. The nuisance calls ended, but we developed a new habit of nonresponse. Now when the phone rings, we never pick up the receiver but call back at our convenience. The analogy with prayer is practically perfect. The typical believer has become accustomed to putting God on hold and returning the call at his convenience. A cartoonist recently speculated how dismayed we would be if the tables were turned and God himself had an answering machine, asking us to leave a message and promising to call back at *his* convenience.

Assuming that we have God's attention and God has ours, we will still encounter difficulty in prayer unless we are clear about whom we are talking with and why we are making the effort. Although prayer inevitably leads to greater conviction, self-awareness is only a happy side effect. The real point of prayer is to know God more intimately, as a prelude to an eternity with him. As our creator, God already knows us better than we know ourselves. In the process of growth through prayer, we will sense change. It will not be God changing, but ourselves.

We pray to a personal God; it is impossible to make friends with an abstraction. God is exclusive and demanding; Christians, Jews, and Moslems are not free to pick and choose among objects of worship as the pagans did. Nevertheless, with the best of intentions, as we conceptualize the object of our prayer we run the risk of trivializing or caricaturing our creator. If, as otherwise faithful believers or honest skeptics, we carry around *childish* concepts of God, then our conversation with God cannot help but be immature. So before we grapple with the technique of prayer, let us afford ourselves a more mature grasp on whom we will be speaking with, beginning with a brief account of God's self-revelation, followed by a brief profile of Jesus, his Son and model of prayer. Lastly, we will note God's Holy Spirit, who (in Paul's words) "intercedes for us with sighs too deep for words" and "searches the hearts of men" (Romans 8:26–27). If we can find the courage to unleash God's Spirit within us, prayer will become almost effortless. God will do it for us.

Does Anyone Believe God?

It has taken me three decades in journalism to appreciate that
God has done a masterful job as a communicator. His revelation is first rate. It took me all that time to be enlightened because I shared the skeptics' suspicion that religion is fabricated
from insufficient and conflicting information. As a believer
myself and a professional communicator all these years, I felt
defensive whenever a doubter challenged God to declare himself clearly. If God wants his way (I acknowledged reluctantly to
myself), why doesn't God show us the way and stop being so
elusive?

Nowadays, in a turnaround, I counter that God is, in fact, an
effective news source, and although he seldom commands
front-page coverage, God nevertheless attracts the attention of
some 95 percent of Americans, who acknowledge him, and notably the 75 percent who admit to praying to God every day. At
length, I have come to the conclusion that, for all our protesta-
tions about God's silence, most of us would prefer a more private God and would be comfortable with less communication
from him. Revelation, after all, is demanding; the more we
know, the more is expected of us.

To better understand God's revelation of himself, let me
confess something basic about the news business: reporters
hate a completely accessible story. They adore exclusives. If you
are not in the news business, you might assume that the way to
reveal something is to hold a press conference and invite
everyone to cover the story. That's because you have seen
White House briefings with all those reporters hanging on
every word and straining to ask a question. In fact, only a few
dozen reporters hang around the White House permanently
and follow the president as an exclusive assignment. Their ostensibly glamorous jobs consist largely of being fed announce-
ments that are more significant for what they conceal than for
what they reveal.

Whenever you see a lot of reporters around, as in a disaster, election, trial, or war, you can bet that what is revealed will be redundant, partial, sanitized, and possibly wrong. Real news is gritty and takes digging by an individual journalist, with information pried from unwilling or unwitting sources. Often getting the real story requires sitting in the lap of danger and putting one's life on the line. In 1988, some three thousand out-of-state reporters invaded Iowa for the presidential caucuses. You may wonder how there could conceivably be three thousand variations on the same story when everyone had the same election results, and you would be right to doubt. There was in fact only one story, and every one of the three thousand reporters got it wrong because they were pressed for instant analysis, which turned out to be faulty.

Pretend for a moment that you are God and want to communicate something. Having nothing whatsoever to hide and wanting everyone's equal attention, you (God) might consider calling a press conference and inviting all comers. From my years in journalism and public relations, I can assure you that the event would be a disappointment, if not an outright fiasco. Reporters hate press conferences for the very reason that you choose to stage one: all the competition is there for the same story. Everyone gets an identical handout. The presentation is controlled; there is no breaking news. Although you allow questions, the answers are predictable, rehearsed, and accessible to everyone. Result: no digging, no dirt, and no story.

Do you think I exaggerate? Surely if the media had a chance to hear you (God) in person, they would turn out, if only from curiosity. Think again. There would be no photo op to attract cameras (God is invisible) and no obvious way to prove that you are who you say you are. Where I worked until recently in Washington, I was just a floor away from the National Press Club, where journalists several times each week host kings and prime ministers, revolutionaries and politicians, generals and assorted celebrities over lunch, after which the prominent visitors state publicly what is on their minds and answer reporters' questions on the record. These revelations of the powerful and famous practically *never* make the news. Why? Precisely because the event is open to everyone.

What Are God's Options?

You can be excused for assuming it should be a cinch for God to communicate. In reality God is required to adopt the methods of every other effective news source—he leaks stories and gives exclusives, often to reluctant reporters (the prophets, apostles, and saints), telling them in effect: "It's your story; now spread the news." Knowing that people are often unmoved by mere words, God stages events (miracles) to capture their attention and to dramatize his meaning. Realizing that we are lulled by prose and bored by instructions, God reverts to poetry and song (the psalms) and to allegory. He reveals himself by telling tales and laces his revelation with parables.

Ben Bradlee, the famed former editor of *The Washington Post,* defines a great news story as one whose revelation draws from the reader an immediate gasp of disbelief followed by shocked comprehension. If Bradlee is correct, then it is understandable that God has chosen to reveal himself in burning bushes, in dreams, floods, and cures, and through people who turn to salt, are swallowed by whales, or emerge live from the tomb still wrapped like mummies. God is only doing his job, capturing everyone's attention so we might be motivated to stick around to listen to what else he may have to say to us personally.

Any newcomer to faith can also be forgiven for assuming that God is a writer, because most believers in the Western world base their faith on the Old and New Testaments and on the Koran, all of them *books.* In point of fact God has never written a word, and Jesus did no more than trace figures in the sand. The scriptures reflect and record only what God has *said* and *done.* Deeds speak louder than words, and God is fundamentally a doer.

A Good Creation

The record of God's self-revelation begins with the book of Genesis, where we learn of his original intention for us. The creation and Eden provide the first clues to those intentions. Let us make ourselves present at the creation and revisit Eden to eavesdrop as the first man and woman walk and converse with their creator:

> Then God said, 'Let us make man in our image . . . Be fruitful and increase, fill the earth and subdue it . . . ' So it was; and God saw all that he had made, and it was very good.
>
> *Genesis 1:26,28,30–31*

It is easy to dismiss the account of creation in Genesis as quaint and mythical. But I recall from my teens the great actor Charles Laughton reading its text from the bare stage of my high school auditorium, where the familiar words became high drama.

Which, of course, the creation was. And it is the first revelation of the character of the God who is the object of our prayer. God created not because he was lonely or bored but to share himself. Before creation there was nothing but God. The account in Genesis is careful to note that God did not shape or manipulate some preexisting material, nor did he shrug off some nonessential part of himself. Rather, God created everything from nothing. We mortals along with all creation sprang from what was originally a void—literally *no*thing.

The consequences of this fact are enormous. People like you and me turn out to be completely God's idea—not part of God, or converted from some earlier and rejected prototype. Men and women are strictly originals: expressions of God's generosity. Nor did God subject his creation to second-guessing. We are not just a divine experiment. Rather, God completed his creation and continues to conserve it. Environmentalists today are anxious to conserve nature and encourage renewable resources, but this is precisely what God achieved at the beginning of time. God gave his creatures the power to reproduce and perpetuate themselves, and he has remained present to sustain everything. The words of the old spiritual still apply: "He's got the whole world in his hands."

From the outset God revealed himself in his creation to be both generous and powerful, but also *sustaining*—which is another word for faithful. It goes without saying that God is anything but impersonal. In the Genesis account God speaks and the universe is formed. But another part of that account is even more telling. Before he took his Sabbath rest, God reviewed everything he had made and declared that "it was very good" (Genesis 1:31). You might expect God to exclaim over his creation, "I made it very well," as an architect would over his monument or an artist over his sculpture. But rather than take personal credit for a job well done, God commends creation itself for the value he originally instilled in it. All of it, God insists, is *good*.

This endorsement is immensely reassuring. When we pray we know not only that we are conversing with a good God, but that we can also be confident that our creator looks upon you and me and our troubled world and pronounces us good. This affirmation is the key to the essential optimism of the Judeo-Christian-Islamic tradition and distinguishes it from those pessimistic faiths and agnosticisms that view life as a corrupt prison from which one's spirit can seek escape only in dissolution. When we open our hearts to God in prayer, we can be certain that he feels at home in us, his creatures. God is not slumming when he abides in his creatures, because he made us, once and for all, *good*. God's Son would underscore this lesson. Jesus scandalized the righteous because he willingly became the guest of sinners, dining in their homes. No one is ever so abject that God does not feel glad to be there, if only we invite him in.

From his Nazi prison, Dietrich Bonhoeffer prayed in confidence on New Year's Day 1945, although he would be executed before the Allied liberation the following spring:

> With every power for good to stay and guide me,
> Comforted and inspired beyond all fear,
> I'll live these days with you in thought beside me,
> And pass, with you, into the coming year.

Conversing in the Garden

In the initial chapter of the first book of the Bible, God already revealed enough about himself to sustain a lifetime of prayer and a desire to spend eternity with him. To my mind God revealed something else, too, about his character: that he is infinitely interesting. Only a God with a sense of adventure and a sense of humor could have fashioned the universe we live in and the ridiculous and wonderful bodies we inhabit. Every fanciful depiction of Noah corralling two of every species in his ark illustrates God's sense of style. Darwin aside, who else but God would endow giraffes with their necks or zebras with their stripes? In his creation God presents his credentials as the ultimate zookeeper, forest ranger, anthropologist, environmentalist, humorist, and (need I add?) artist and architect of the universe.

I recall that when the film actor George Sanders killed himself, he left a letter that gave boredom with life as his excuse—this despite tolerable good health, a handsome appearance, and a glamorous life. In Western religious tradition, suicide is deemed the ultimate sin because it is the rejection of God and all of God's creation, beginning with one's own life. Consider that two of Jesus' closest friends, Judas and Peter, each betrayed him: Judas by delivering Jesus to the authorities for thirty pieces of silver, and Peter by denying three times that he even knew Jesus. But history has come to judge Peter a hero and Judas a villain. The distinction is that Peter in his guilt sought forgiveness and affirmed life, whereas Judas despaired and obliterated his life.

Creation was the initial adventure that made all subsequent stories possible. The first of those adventures came with God's creation of man and woman. From the Genesis account Adam and Eve appear to be simple souls, but not thereby innocent. Genesis relates that our parents by day tilled the garden of Eden, then walked and conversed with God in the cool of the evening. In an extraordinary act of trust, God gave this couple total dominion and care over all the creatures in their peaceable kingdom.

What did they talk to God about? I suspect they, like gardeners ever after, conversed about crops and complained about critters. What we know for certain from Genesis is that God gave them one piece of strict advice: do not eat the fruit of the tree of the knowledge of good and evil. I beg your forbearance if the Genesis account appears outlandish; it is actually more subtle than it seems. What on earth could this naive couple have made of their creator's warning about good and evil when they were surrounded exclusively by God's good creation? How could they even conceive of evil, let alone be tempted to taste the knowledge of it? In the story, Satan, appearing as a serpent, supplies the answer. Recall from Milton's *Paradise Lost* that Satan, himself a creature, had *created* evil by declaring his independence of his creator. Now he sought company in his isolation by seducing God's newest creatures—man and woman—to declare their independence as well. It was a choice that Satan knew full well was foredoomed, inasmuch as it was based on the pretense that the creature is the equal of the creator. "You shall be as gods, knowing good and evil," the Prince of Liars insinuates. A later Jewish proverb has it that "the mouth bites the hand that feeds it." This is precisely how sin entered into the world. The man and woman tired of God's generosity and resolved to make it on their own and, if possible, to go into competition with their tiresome maker.

The Genesis story suggests that God expelled Adam and Eve from the garden; in fact, they exiled themselves by their declaration of independence. Here was the rare instance in which God and Satan agreed. Given the knowledge of good and evil, mankind as often as not will choose evil.

The Covenant

Despite their unavailing attempts to reassign blame ("The woman enticed me!" "The serpent made me do it!"), our now-exiled parents were not abandoned by their creator. According to the biblical account, they were given long lives and children, but after the original sin there was no recovery of lost innocence. In envy, their son Cain murdered his brother, Abel. And eventually, after countless generations of escalating willfulness, the story relates of humankind that God "was sorry that he had ever made them and put them on the earth." In a radical move to reform his creation, God caused a great flood that swallowed all but the righteous Noah and his family, plus a pair of every living species, so that, once the waters receded, a new beginning might be made. A rainbow heralded the new start, and God made a covenant to sustain his creation.

Sustain it God did, but amnesia soon set in, and God was forgotten by his creatures, supplanted by deities who were products of desperation and feverish imagination and could answer humankind's prayers only with silence. Then, less than two millennia before the birth of Christ, the silence was shattered. Unbidden, a message came from God. He spoke to Abraham, a nomad, directing him to travel between the Mediterranean and the Jordan, there to dominate the land and father a new people, who would inherit the earth. He would later identify himself as the one god, Yahweh—"I am who am"—but initially he presented himself as Abraham's own God and crafted a covenant with the patriarch and his descendants that confirmed in effect:

> I am your god;
> you are my people.
> If you will be faithful to me,
> I will be faithful to you.

From this moment, religion was no longer the product of superstition, fear, and yearning following the expulsion from Eden, but returned to the trusting relationship of God and humanity. God had reentered history and had summoned humankind to enter into a covenant. There was no longer any need to discover God; God had found us.

When Yahweh announced himself to Abraham as the one true God, the patriarch-to-be was abandoned by his kindred, who remained pagans. For the rest of his life Abraham wandered in the promised land preaching his faith, then finally died in exile as founder of a new people chosen to carry God's message to mankind. They were called Jews, named after Abraham's great-grandson, Judah.

Tests for Faithfulness

The price of being thus chosen would be unrelenting tests for fidelity. Abraham himself was tested to prove whether he loved God more than his own son, who was his most precious gift from God. Ordered to sacrifice Isaac, Abraham was restrained by God only at the last moment of trial.

God's covenant demanded reciprocity. Man and woman must serve God by imitating God's ways. As God is just and merciful, so we must be fair and loving. The great commandment given through Moses was this: You shall love the Lord your God with all your heart, with all your might, and with all your soul. The covenant was sealed through the sign of circumcision. Every Jewish male was to bear this mark, associated with his powers of reproduction, as a reminder that God was the ultimate life-giver and sustainer.

The tests were relentless. Having moved to Egypt and finding themselves enslaved, Abraham's descendants were led back to the land of promise by Moses in the Exodus and briefly knew glory under Solomon and David. But there would be a long exile—to Babylon—and for centuries the people of the promised land would be at the almost constant mercy of their stronger neighbors. At length, sixty-three years before the birth of Jesus, the Roman general Pompey conquered Jerusalem, in the process slaughtering twelve thousand Jews, and annexed the promised land as a small ghetto in a vast pagan empire.

Why would a faithful God allow his chosen people to suffer? In Second Isaiah the prophet suggested an answer in its reference to a Suffering Servant. Christians would identify the Servant with Jesus, suffering for sin on the cross; but at the time many Jews felt it referred to the entire Jewish nation, carrying not only the burden of its own transgressions, but the sins of all peoples. This, they surmised, was the cost of their special adoption by God. Elsewhere in the Bible, Job acknowledged his inability to comprehend God's providence and simply accepted his personal misery. What we do understand is that suffering tested the nation's faith. Resignation, not comprehension, motivates this Hasidic prayer:

> God, do not tell me why I suffer,
> For I am no doubt unworthy to know why,
> But help me to believe that I suffer for your sake!

Seeking a new source of hope, the Jews began to anticipate a savior, a messiah with power to restore independence and inaugurate an era of peace and justice. To fulfill these great expectations, the messiah would have to be a politician and general as well as spiritual leader.

What Jesus Reveals About God

As it happened, the messiah appeared inauspiciously: a babe in swaddling clothes born in a barn, the son of an obscure couple from a provincial village in the tiny defeated nation. At the age of thirty he began a brief public life. He wrote nothing that has survived, held no office, spoke from no public platform, led no army. He never left his homeland. No one bothered to note his appearance for posterity. He spoke to no more than a few thousand men, women, and children, most of them citizens of no distinction. Within three years he was dead, executed as a common criminal. Yet twenty centuries later the world reckons each year as "the year of our Lord." It is as if time itself began with the birth of Jesus. This prompted Isaac Watts to proclaim the familiar carol—

> Joy to the world! The Lord is come;
> Let earth receive her King.
> Let ev'ry heart prepare him room,
> And heaven and nature sing.

—and Charles Wesley (John's brother) to pray in simplicity:

> Gentle Jesus, meek and mild,
> Look upon a little child;
> Pity my simplicity,
> Suffer me to come to thee.

Jesus was a Jew. He spoke to Jews, in terms they uniquely understood, of the one good God, creator of the universe, who chose humankind for his love and sealed a covenant of mutual faith. In the gospel accounts, the adult Jesus makes his first appearance at the river Jordan, where he submits to baptism by his cousin John. The ritual of washing was understood to signify repentance, but it was clear to John that Jesus was without sin. Only later would it emerge that God intended Jesus to assume personally the burden of everyone else's sins.

"He went about doing good," the gospel relates, but Jesus refused to make a spectacle of his power. Instead, he spoke clearly and forcefully in terms even a child could understand

and act upon. Jesus did not speculate or philosophize. He taught, explained, and insisted with total authority. For Jesus, God's pervasive presence and fatherly love, God's power and righteousness, mercy and goodness were not just options, but compelling permanent facts of experience. Communion with God was, for Jesus, a conscious reality accessible to every man, woman, and child.

At Jesus' baptism, God himself confirmed Jesus' ministry: "This is my beloved Son; my favor rests on him." Jesus, in turn, called God "Father," not in the narrow sense of creator, but as his own loving father and ours. When Jesus prayed, he called God "Abba" with the same familiarity as we call our human fathers "Dad" or "Daddy." In his parable of the prodigal son, Jesus explained the kind of father God is. In Jesus' story, the father runs to meet his wayward son, embracing and kissing him, and prepares a feast to celebrate his return to the family. This is the God whom Jesus knew and emulated—a Father who loves and forgives with unrelenting generosity. Jesus asserted: when you see me, you see the Father. God's love is indiscriminate. And Jesus loved just as indiscriminately, dying for everyone.

God's Inner Life

This, then, is the God to whom we pray. God is the voice at the other end of the eternal conversation between creature and creator. God has spoken through the ages, and he will speak again to us if we will be still and listen with our hearts.

Earlier I noted that God is self-sufficient; he created us not from loneliness or need but from love. When we affirm that "God is love," we reflect only indirectly on his concern for his creatures. Instead we refer to God's *inner* life, independent of his creation. Christianity affirms that the one God is not only Father, but also Son and Spirit. How one God can be a Trinity is perhaps the greatest mystery of faith. But setting perplexities aside, the affirmation of God's inner life enriches our sense of the creator. God is not solitary at all, but a partnership and a family. The Son loves the Father; the Spirit *is* that love. It is this Spirit who dwells in you and me, enabling us to carry on the conversation that is prayer. Indeed, as Saint Paul affirmed, it is God's own Spirit within us who carries on our part of the eternal conversation—if we allow him.

King George VI broadcast this prayerful message to the British people on the outbreak of the Second World War:

> I said to the man who stood at the gate of the year: "Give me a light that I may tred safely into the unknown." And he replied: "Go out into the darkness and put your hand into the hand of God. That shall be to you better than light and safer than a known way."

4
Starting the Conversation

"Common people do not pray; they only beg."

George Bernard Shaw, *Misalliance*

Although I have always loved music, after sixty years on the planet I still cannot read a note, whereas my wife has studied, composed, performed, and taught music since the age of eight. Daily our home reverberates with music from the Stieff grand piano that is its focus, while my virtuoso abilities are restricted to humming, whistling, and singing Sinatra in the shower and hymns in church. My love of music does not obscure the fact that, musically, I am a primitive.

Although it is clear that we pray as spontaneously as we hum a tune, spontaneity is not prayer's chief virtue. Rather, spontaneity is a temptation to let well enough alone when our prayer is not well enough at all, but only a periodic swelling of the heart or an occasional cry for help. Just as it is vastly more important for me to love God than for me to love music, it is essential for me to communicate with God better than I sing, since that is what I am destined to do eternally. I can go to my grave musically illiterate with mere regret, but I cannot hum and whistle my way through life into the presence of God. Rather, I must *learn* to pray effectively, which takes discipline but promises enormous dividends from the outset.

Your prayer need not be contrived to be thoughtful. From

his best-selling book of the sixties, *Are You Running With Me, Jesus?* here is the Reverend Malcolm Boyd's prayer to begin his day:

> It's morning, Jesus. It's morning, and here's that light and sound all over again. I've got to move fast . . . get into the bathroom, wash up, grab a bite to eat, and run some more. I just don't feel like it, Lord. What I really want to do is to get back into bed, pull up the covers, and sleep. All I seem to want today is the big sleep, and here I've got to run all over again. Where am I running? You know these things I can't understand. It's not that I need to have you tell me. What counts most is just that somebody knows, and it's you. That helps a lot. So I'll follow along, okay? But lead, Lord. Now I've got to run. Are you running with me, Jesus?

The Curse of Creativity

Regrettably, much of what goes by the label of personal prayer is little more than an invitation to God to listen in on our free-association conversations with ourselves. We are like a child who randomly picks notes on a keyboard in the hope of coming up with a melody. The greatest impediment to effective prayer is an inflated valuation of creativity. It is as if we advised a beginning piano student to practice only music of her own composition, or a young dancer to act exclusively as her own choreographer. Logically extended, the contemporary obsession with creativity would lead us to expect each aspiring athlete to become proficient only in games of his own creation or an actor to learn his craft exclusively in plays he has written.

In fact musicians become proficient by playing exercises, dancers spend countless hours at the barre, skaters practice school figures, and athletes repeat the fundamentals of their sport over and over again. If every actor insisted on being his own playwright, we would never see Shakespeare.

Prayer, the most important exercise of our lives (as well as the principal occupation of eternity) requires similar practice, application, and attention, in full knowledge that no one (least of all God) is judging or scoring us as in sports and the arts. Admittedly, the object of prayer is not conversation at all but the intimate knowledge of God, which is beyond words. Yet inasmuch as beginners must start with words (if only to graduate beyond them), we need to choose our words well, and they will probably not be the first that come to mind.

At the outset, let us combat the temptation to be instant prodigies of prayer and begin by learning the language of prayer through familiarizing ourselves with its classics. At the end of this book, there are many prayers that have withstood the test of time and are yours to use without fear of transgressing copyright. Just as no audience would be offended if you played Chopin rather than music of your own composition, God will not mind if you wrap your sentiments in others' words. When the apostles asked Jesus to teach them to pray, he did not counsel them to be creative; rather, he gave them the Lord's Prayer, which has proved serviceable for two thousand years and has not lost its warranty.

Another Language

When I went to Paris as a theological student in the sixties I had only two years of high school French to support my attempts to understand and be understood by the natives and my teachers. Having been raised in ethnic neighborhoods in Chicago, I was prone to patronize immigrants with inadequate English and Old World accents. Now I was the one with the accent, faulty grammar, and inadequate vocabulary. Of necessity, I stumbled along and eventually made myself understood, in the full realization that every time I opened my mouth I sounded as if I had just got off the boat. Although fluency in French eludes me to this day, I made progress in the language and made friends besides.

Prayer is a different language, even when its words are in

English. The closest equivalent to prayer is poetry, whose meaning is something other than the literal sense of the words. Poetry employs rhyme and meter with an economy of words to perform its function as art: to distill experience to its essence, to free and expand the spirit, and to focus one's attention. For example, the death of his friend John Keats impelled Shelley to write this prayerful verse in *Adonais:*

> The One remains, the many change and pass;
> Heaven's light forever shines, Earth's shadows fly;
> Life, like a dome of many-colored glass,
> Stains the white radiance of Eternity . . .
> That Light whose smile kindles the Universe,
> That Beauty in which all things work and move,
> That Benediction which the eclipsing Curse
> of birth can quench not, that sustaining Love
> Which through the web of being blindly wove
> By man and beast and earth and air and sea,
> Burns bright or dim, as each are mirrors of
> The Fire for which all thirst . . .

If you are put off by my analogy between poetry and prayer, reflect that popular songs would fall flat if their lines failed to rhyme. Even the emptiest lyric is enhanced by the disciplines of rhyme and rhythm. So with prayer. If I were dining with the queen I would make certain in advance that I had something to say, not simply rely on blurting out the banalities of my day. To be sure, God is no snob, but prayer is an elevating experience, not a coffee klatch. In prayer we are meeting our maker, not our maid, so the conversation deserves dignity and discipline.

Now to practical matters. I have already answered the "who" and "why" of prayer, but the standard journalistic queries of "what," "when," "where," and "how" still need to be addressed.

What to Say

Pious schoolchildren are taught that there are four kinds of prayer, summarized by the mnemonic formula ACTS, namely, adoration, contrition, thanksgiving, and supplication. I have always suspected that those stuffy polysyllables were deliberately chosen to make the formula work, rather than the other way around. Nevertheless, they denote the four basic approaches to God, which can be expressed in these terms:

"You're wonderful—I love you."
"I'm sorry."
"Thank you."
"Please."

Stated this simply, prayer is stunningly similar to the habits we attempt to instill in every polite child, trusting that he or she will take them into adulthood. If we seriously believe ourselves when we refer to God as our *Father,* then these sentiments are not at all childish, but only realistic acknowledgments of our dependency and our confidence.

"You're wonderful—I love you."

Orthodox Jews begin their day with the Eighteen Benedictions, praising God for who he is and what he has done. Here is Psalm 150, illustrating the first approach to prayer. Earlier in our century it was set to music by Igor Stravinsky in his *Symphony of Psalms:*

O praise God in his sanctuary; praise him in the firmament of his power.
Praise him in his noble acts; praise him according to his excellent greatness.
Praise him in the sound of the trumpet; praise him upon the

lute and harp.
Praise him in the timbrels and dances; praise him upon the
strings and pipe.
Praise him upon the well-tuned cymbals; praise him upon the
loud cymbals.
Let every thing that hath breath praise the Lord.

The ancient psalms, associated with King David, are princi-
pally poems of praise. Similarly, the great hymns, notably the
Te Deum ("We praise thee as God") are those that exalt God.

Rest assured, prayers of praise are not exercises in flattery.
God knows all about himself and does not need to be reas-
sured by us. If anything, prayers of praise flatter the person
who prays, since they acknowledge the sort of God who created and sustains us. As the pageantry of the queen's corona-
tion is designed not to impress the queen but her subjects, so
prayers of praise remind us of the grandeur of God, in whose
image we were made.

But note that we do not stop with telling God he is wonderful. We follow up with what God truly wants to hear: that we
love him. Consider the simple sentiment of Christina Rossetti:

> What can I give Him,
> Poor as I am?
> If I were a shepherd,
> I would bring a lamb,
> If I were a Wise Man,
> I would do my part,—Yet what can I give Him?
> Give my heart.

The history of the world can be read as the unrequited love
of the faithful creator for his creatures. A parent does not
merely want his child to be respectful, grateful, and courteous;
he wants him to be loving. That is the fulfillment of the prayer
of praise. Yet love cannot be commanded, as many a sad suitor
can attest. God gives us the power to disregard him and even

dismiss him. But to know God is to love him, and the reverse is equally true. The more we know him and acknowledge him in praise, the deeper our love will become.

The grandeur of God does not require that our prayers be grand. Here, for example, is the humble prayer of my friend and mentor Donald Coggan, 101st archbishop of Canterbury:

> Lord Jesus, I don't know much about you,
> But I am willing to learn;
> And I am ready to give all that I know of myself
> To all that I know of you;
> And I am willing to go on learning.

"I'm sorry."

My basic training in faith came from nuns, who attempted to persuade me that God's ego is extremely fragile. By their calculation, the divinity was offended by everything from my gum chewing to my slouch while kneeling. The sacred host was to be consumed neatly without chewing for, after all, what child could presume to bite his creator!

In retrospect, I recognize that the sisters were only attempting to instill courtesy in this rude boy, and I took their lesson to heart. To this day I bow to the cross as a mark of respect and tip my hat when I pass a church—but not because I believe God to be a prima donna. If revelation is clear about anything, it is that God has been putting up with a lot of grief from his creatures from the beginning but has not given up on them. A lovely Christmas carol acknowledges that God's Son died "for poor, ornery children like you and like I," which illustrates the lengths the Father has gone to forgive.

Yet even God cannot forgive offenses for which we are not sorry. Forgiveness is readily available, but God's response requires our initiative. When a criminal throws himself on the mercy of the court, he may win an easing of his sentence. But a hardened or indifferent criminal can hardly expect mercy when he refuses to request it.

There is little we can do to offend God directly and nothing to really hurt him. Blasphemy and idolatry may have been problems in the past but now are rare. Only rejection and indifference shut God out. Indirectly, of course, we offend God by our mistreatment of his creation—the world, our fellowmen, and ourselves. Environmentalists do not necessarily revere nature as God's creation, but they insist that it be conserved and respected. Believers have even better reason to revere nature: it is God's.

In our century neurotic guilt has become so widespread that it threatens to obscure real sin. Sentimentality and good intentions have numbed our moral sensibilities. It has become sufficient to plead: "Don't expect me to be perfect." But sin cannot be identified as imperfection; Jesus was clear about this when he affirmed that only God is good. Sin is real and (contrary to popular belief) rarely provides pleasure. Rather, sin is a perverse way of making our own lives and those of our fellow creatures miserable.

If like many others you are unaccustomed to thinking in terms of sin and cannot imagine how you might have hurt anyone, ask a friend or a colleague to give you the polite lowdown on yourself. For that matter, ask a loved one whether you are taking sufficient care of yourself. Sin starts with our irresponsibility toward ourselves; we are the principal victims of our own abuse.

Those who pray from *The Book of Common Prayer* ask forgiveness not only for the hurtful things they have done but "for things left undone." Day in and day out indifference causes more suffering than all the world's crimes taken together. Politicians of all stripes flog formulas for cutting the crime rate. But if public policy were successful in eliminating crime altogether, there would still be sin in the world, consisting of humankind's needs that go unanswered by reason of indifference. No one who prays can be indifferent.

Here is Saint Augustine's confession:

> O Lord, the house of my soul is narrow;
> enlarge it that you may enter in.
> It is ruinous, O repair it!
> It displeases your sight; I confess it, I know.
> But who shall cleanse it, to whom shall I cry but to you?

"Thank you."

It is easy to develop the habit of expressing gratitude. At the end of each day when I left my office, I made a point of thanking my coworkers for what they had accomplished. But more often than not, I was vague about what they had toiled over, so my thanks were perfunctory—little more than manners learned from my parents.

Gratitude is more than politeness; it is rooted in reality. Thanksgiving is based on the recognition of one's blessings, which are manifold. Ironically, the very quantity and variety of our blessings make them difficult to count and easy to take for granted. In America we set aside but one day in 365 for purposes of thanksgiving. Monks, Jews, and Moslems are more realistic, waking each day to sing God's praises and to thank him for his generosity. Rabbi Larry Kushner relates that he has learned to marvel each morning that his body is whole, his mind is functioning, and he can stand up and move. Only when the most routine things are regarded rightly as gifts can we pray in thanksgiving. Perversely, we usually thank God for sight only when we see a blind person or for our health when we happen to confront an invalid. We need to savor our blessings as we would a good meal. Instead we devour them thoughtlessly like fast food.

Revelation is clear that there are no fast blessings. From the dawn of creation, men and women acknowledged this fact by spontaneously offering sacrifices, less to propitiate the diety than to acknowledge him as the source of all they possessed. Sophisticated moderns shudder at the notion of slaying a sacrificial animal and judge it pointless to offer crops to one's creator; yet these primitive rites were powerful gestures acknowledging the source of all life and nourishment. The point of sacrifice is not destruction but clarity of mind. When Jesus went out to pray, he retreated into the desert and fasted, not in the spirit of sacrifice, but to clear away the rubble of distraction. You and I may be unable to find a convenient desert for our prayer, but we can seek out a simple setting, where we can see the sun, moon, and stars, sense our breathing, and confront the wonder of life, which is a gift prefiguring what is in store for us eternally. In acknowledging creation, we draw closer to its creator, which after all is the principal point of prayer.

"Please."

In one respect, asking for favors is the easiest form of prayer, but in the final analysis proves to be the hardest. On the face of it, each of us is the world's unchallenged authority on what we want, but we haven't a clue whether what we want is God's will or will be good for us. Even when we ask for what seems to be equally in God's interest and ours (peace, knowledge, love, justice), we lack perspective on how our wishes fit into the bigger picture. If I pray for fair weather for a wedding and the farmer prays for rain for his harvest, only one of us will get his way. Short of a miracle, God cannot satisfy both our requests, which are equally legitimate. In the old days, Protestants and Catholics, Jews and Moslems all prayed to the same God to favor them against the others. With the perspective of time, we now have to wonder whether any of these prayers was a legitimate call on God to take sides. So what seems to be certain (what we want) turns out to be speculative (what God intends). We are on much more solid ground when we offer God our praise, love, sorrow, and gratitude. Those overtures God clearly deserves and will respond to.

Rest assured, nothing here denigrates the prayer of petition. We merely acknowledge that we do not grasp the shape of providence. Nevertheless, we are safe in calling on that providence, confident that God has our best interests at heart. As Jesus confirmed in his Sermon on the Mount, "Look at the birds in the sky. They never sow nor reap nor store away in barns, and yet your heavenly Father feeds them." He asks, "Aren't you more valuable to him than they are? . . . Set your heart on his kingdom and his goodness, and all these things will come to you as a matter of course. Don't worry at all about tomorrow. Tomorrow can take care of itself!" (Matthew 6:26, 33–34).

When and Where to Pray

Two basic questions remain to be answered: when and where shall I pray? They can be answered in tandem. If you are a believer, in all likelihood you do your serious praying in church once a week and your daily praying on the run or before you retire at day's end. I follow this pattern myself, not from design but from habit, and concede it has serious shortcomings. Praying in church is something as distinct from personal prayer as team play is from individual sports or ensemble performance is from solo musicianship. Communal worship is the love of God expressed within the family of faith, whereas personal prayer is akin to the intimacy of two close friends or lovers.

Private prayer does not usurp public worship but complements it. In church we pray and sing together with friends and strangers alike, relying on ritual to acknowledge our common God and our responsibilities to one another. Worship in common recognizes God's penchant for working with groups. God acts corporately, first choosing Noah's family, then the Jews, finally embracing the Gentiles as well. To underscore God's preference, Jesus promised that wherever two or three persons are gathered in his name, he will be present to them. Accordingly, our relationship to God is simultaneously public and private. Communal worship benefits from ritual and the participation of others, whereas in personal prayer we are on our own. How shall we proceed in this solitary enterprise?

"Be still and know that I am God," the psalmist counsels, and the poet T. S. Eliot adds, "Teach us to care and not to care; teach us to sit still." You and I can conceivably pray to God on the run—praising, loving, and thanking him, repenting and asking for assistance. But that makes only for a monologue and precludes God from joining the conversation. To hear God's voice, we need to set aside sufficient time and solitude every day to drop our guard, filter the static of daily living, and flush out our frenzy. This will be easier for some than for others. It involves simultaneously letting go and paying attention, which on the face of it may appear contradictory. Our experience is that relaxation ultimately leads to sleep, whereas attention requires the focusing of energy. In practice, cultivating a passive attitude opens the mind and heart to God and allows us to concentrate on him rather than on ourselves.

That passivity and attention are not incompatible can be illustrated by two distinctly different experiences: suggestion and sex. The object of hypnotism is to place a subject in a trancelike state so he or she is open to suggestion. Barriers are breached; passivity opens the way to communication in a deep motivating sense that can actually change one's outlook and behavior. In sexual ecstasy we focus intense attention on sensation at the same time as we are passive to the person we love. Excitement leads to peace, but attention never flags.

Serendipity

The practice of prayer has serendipitous side effects that are attractive in themselves but should not be allowed to obscure the single object of prayer, which is intimacy with God. Like transcendental meditation, autosuggestion, and visualization, the practice of prayer can

—focus attention
—bring clarity of mind
—relieve anxiety and pain
—lower blood pressure
—free judgment from emotion
—spread calm to the rest of your life

The techniques behind effective prayer can even help you drop unhealthy habits and assume healthy ones. They can relieve insomnia, lower allergic reactions, and even help you lose weight. But I hasten to add that these attractions are *not the products of prayer itself* or God's reward to us for taking the trouble to get in touch with him. Yogis using similar techniques can accomplish more in terms of physical and mental control than you or I, but they are not necessarily praying. It is just as well to acknowledge this at the outset to forestall any temptation to feel smug when the quality of our lives improves after we develop the habit of prayer. It will be neither our virtue nor God's favor that accounts for the enhancement, but simply the effect of the exercise discipline that underlies prayer.

Achieving the Prayerful State

Prayer is not like ordinary conversation over the phone or across the dinner table. Talk is cheap and automatic, whereas prayer requires preparation. In this respect, it is more like writing a letter—a love letter to be sure. To attempt a letter I need materials, a place to sit, and the quiet and solitude to concentrate attention. When I write, I choose my words and expressions more judiciously, rather than babble about whatever happens to be on my mind or on my nerves.

To achieve a prayerful state you must begin not by talking to

God but *to yourself.* You will talk yourself into prayer and visualize your progress. By narrowing your attention, you will pay greater attention. How many rainbows have you missed in life because you did not look up? From now on you will see every rainbow because you will be expecting them. In her poem "Pity," Sara Teasdale converts her mourning for lost love into a prayer:

> They never saw my lover's face,
> They only know our love was brief,
> Wearing awhile a windy grace
> And passing like an autumn leaf.
>
> They wonder why I do not weep,
> They think it strange that I can sing,
> They say, "Her love was scarcely deep
> Since it left so slight a sting."
>
> They never saw my love, nor knew
> That in my heart's most secret place
> I pity them as angels do
> Men who have never seen God's face.

The alchemy of prayer is such that every human emotion (save despair) can expand your spirit and increase your discernment. You will begin to see God's face in the unlikeliest corners of his creation.

The word for placing oneself in a prayerful state is "recollection." It amounts to nothing more complicated than telling yourself what you are going to do and concentrating your attention. It may help to read a favorite passage from scripture, a psalm, or a poem—not for analysis but as a pretext for shutting out distractions that have nothing whatsoever to do with the conversation that is prayer. Once you actually begin praying you will find you no longer need the words that helped you acquire this mental focus. In fact, if you cling to them, *they* will become distractions. Remember, your aim is not to read about God or think about him, but to converse with him. You want, insofar as it is possible this side of eternity, to meet God face-to-face. Even then you do not want to dominate the conversation (you can listen to yourself any time). Rather, you want to open yourself to God and let him speak to you in a language of his choosing, even if that language sounds very much like silence. For centuries Quakers have continued to gather in their meeting houses, each of them open to inspiration, undeterred if the sky neglects to open every time.

Just as a glance or a sigh is sufficient communication for lovers, the message conveyed in prayer is ultimately inexpressible in words. God's voice will not sound like Charlton Heston's, nor is God likely to direct you to raise an army to defend the dauphin. The immediate aim of prayer is to establish the *presence* of the God you love, not to receive a message. Like many another uxorious husband, I am content just knowing my wife is around, even when she is preoccupied with something or someone other than me. God does better: he is always prepared to be preoccupied with you.

What you will be developing is a facility for *contemplation,* or *contemplative prayer.* Unfortunately, "contemplation" is an equivocal term that suggests deep thought and reminds one of Rodin's statue of *The Thinker,* elbow on knee, chin in hand, pondering life's mysteries. That is not at all what you are after. When experts pray, they discard thinking altogether in favor of passive attention. They are known as "contemplatives." Your practice with oral and mental prayers of praise, sorrow, gratitude, and petition has already prepared you for contemplative prayer, but once you have pronounced them, it is time now for you to fall silent so God can speak.

To accomplish your objective you will need a place free of distractions, a passive attitude, a focus for your attention, and sufficient time. You will also need patience with yourself.

A Place Free of Distractions

Once upon a time I read that Wall Street stockbrokers of every faith find Trinity Church a haven for prayer in the midst of a trading day. One day, early for an appointment at the New York Stock Exchange, I had my cab drop me at the church, where I spent half an hour only halfheartedly praying. I found myself distracted by the beauty of the church and its LaFarge windows. I reluctantly concluded, "I can pray anytime, but when will I see this magnificence again?"

In contemplative prayer you are going to close your eyes, so it doesn't matter where you are as long as it is free of things that happen to distract *you*. My wife comments on my zombielike ability to write and think on planes, trains, and my commuter bus to Washington. A secret: I carry earplugs in my pocket everywhere day and night and often use them. Only you know what distracts you: a baby's cry, the noise of traffic, a cat scratching at the bedroom door, a cake baking in the oven, a phone that may ring at any time. When you begin contemplative prayer, insofar as it is possible choose the same time and same place each day, so they become identified as your prayer time and place. During long years of insomnia, I encountered the consistent counsel of sleep researchers to set aside one's bed strictly for sleeping, so it is identified exclusively as a place for rest—not an all-purpose platform for TV watching, popcorn eating, dog petting, conversation, and lovemaking. Although it will seem artificial to you at the outset, you will need to construct a personal "chapel" exclusively for contemplative prayer. Friends from large families often tell me the only place they can be alone is the bathroom. If that is your situation, your bathroom may be your chapel.

A Passive Attitude

For all my ability to ignore distractions, I am at heart a control freak, ever fearful that without my constant intervention the earth might slip off its axis. Alas, fussbudgetry has no place in prayer, just as emotional manipulation has no place in a loving relationship. The myth that men are aggressors and women passive receptors in intimate relations has long since been exploded. Neither sex is dominant, but men and women are equally inclined to seek a measure of control to protect themselves from being hurt or abandoned emotionally.

Control is essentially a defensive posture and is pointless in prayer. It is the enemy of passive attention. God is totally trustworthy; he will never abandon you. God knows you better than you know yourself, and your destiny is eternity with him. You are praying now in anticipation of that destiny. You can let go in perfect confidence.

As we will see in detail later, the traditional postures for prayer combine symbolism and practicality. Early Christians prayed standing, following the straightforward Jewish example. In the Dark Ages, Irish monks extended their arms in the manner of Christ on the cross. Kneeling as a posture for prayer took its cue from the obeisance of the feudal vassal to his temporal lord. Christian monks in choir were allowed to sit from time to time in their stalls during the Divine Office, but only on narrow ledges. In each instance the person at prayer assumed a posture that could be held for a time without discomfort and without the risk of falling asleep. To this day Japanese sit on their heels during prayer; elsewhere in the East the lotus position is favored for contemplative prayer. Most Westerners find these postures uncomfortable and therefore distracting.

In contemplative prayer you will want to find the most comfortable position consistent with staying awake and paying attention. A straight-backed chair is usually best. Seated with eyes closed, head resting squarely on your neck and shoulders, hands resting loosely in your lap, tongue touching the roof of your mouth, breathing quietly through your nose, you will be both comfortable and alert.

Sufficient Time

You will want to work your way up to at least one uninterrupted twenty-minute session each day. More time is not necessarily better; however, only those who have mastered contemplative prayer slip quickly into full concentrated passivity. The rest of us will spend many minutes clearing our heads of distractions, so we need that extra time. When you add a few moments for preliminary reading and mental prayer before emptying your mind and focusing on God, the ideal time requirement will be closer to half an hour. That may seem like a lot of time, but not compared to the usual forty minutes' daily aerobic exercise prescribed by health specialists. Contemplative prayer delivers mental and physical benefits besides its principal goal, so the set-aside of twenty to thirty minutes daily is not excessive. With practice, you will develop facility and gain more from shorter and more frequent periods of prayer.

Focused Attention

You want to make your prayer as natural and unforced as breathing. You can accomplish that by tying your prayer to every breath you take, silently repeating the same words or phrases with every inhalation and exhalation. Choose the words that best express your overture to God—the simpler and shorter the better. The famed Jesus Prayer of the desert monks was: (*inhale*) "Lord Jesus Christ" (*exhale*) "have mercy on me, a sinner." I find those to be a lot of words for one breath cycle, but it suited them. A Christian might prefer a simpler prayer: (*inhale*) "My Jesus" (*exhale*) "I love you." Jews or Moslems will choose brief sentiments more relevant to their faiths. A truth-seeking skeptic might pray: (*inhale*) "I believe" (*exhale*) "Help my unbelief."

Contemplative prayer is not the property of any religious tradition and is as old as any of them. Accordingly, the words you choose are of much less importance than your sincerity and calm persistence in repetition. In any case, after a brief time the words will lose their meaning and be reduced to the elements of sound. That is precisely what you want to happen, because then the words themselves will cease to be distractions; you will cease analyzing and thinking, and start concentrating. In short, you will be attending to God, not to words.

Instead of employing brief, repetitive prayers, practitioners of transcendental meditation choose mantras, consisting of foreign phrases or sounds with no meaning whatsoever. Their rationale: the less meaning, the better. If you find that the words you choose for your meditative prayer have become distractions themselves, opt for something simpler. The first generation of Christians used the Aramaic word *maranatha,* meaning "Come, Lord."

Whatever words you choose, remain faithful to them throughout your whole session. Rest assured, there is no magic formula that summons God like a genie from a lamp. Do not become enamored of technique. The only function of repetition is to foster your passive attention so you will lower your mental and emotional barriers, open the door to your heart, and sense God's presence. God needs no persuasion whatsoever to join you; rather, you must persuade yourself that you want him. That takes practice.

Patience with Yourself

The hardest thing in the world is to do absolutely nothing. Even couch potatoes are chronically occupied or preoccupied. Unless we are in a coma, our waking hours are filled with tasks and worries. Even when we relax, we tend to daydream, and in stress we may hallucinate. In sleep we dream. At work we worry. In love we keep score. In the midst of play I find myself asking, "Am I having fun yet?"

Accordingly, when we propose to practice contemplative

prayer, we are inclined to approach it as an activity, ask for our instructions, and expect a payoff. We approach prayer as if it were an appliance: plug it in and see if it works. Unfortunately, the practice of prayer runs contrary to all our predispositions. In contemplative prayer you will be like a solitary fisherman in a flat-bottomed boat drifting on a placid lake. Once you have set out your lines, there is nothing to do but wait and be content, even if you catch nothing this day. A frenzied fisherman will be tempted to recover his lines, change his bait, row to a more promising part of the lake, start casting and reeling or trolling, then declare the day a failure if the fish aren't biting. By contrast, a true fisherman loves fishing, whatever the catch. A true contemplative loves praying even when God seems silent.

Years ago, when I moved my family beyond Washington's Capital Beltway to a little lakeside house in the Virginia forest, my wife presented me with a magnificent red canoe and fishing gear. In eight years, I am embarrassed to admit, the boat has been in the water perhaps a dozen times, and the rod and reel are still cocooned in their Styrofoam and shrink-wrap. Until I totally retire, the fish of Lake Montclair have nothing to fear from this presumptive sportsman, because I do not as yet have the leisure or mind to pursue them.

But I do have time for contemplative prayer, and so do you, because it fits into a busy life and nourishes it. As you practice regularly—concentrating on the few words of your prayer, repeating them with every breath you take—you will find your respiration slows, and you will become increasingly calm. You will also find your attention wandering. That is natural, so if something itches, scratch it, then return to your routine. The very first time I attempted waterskiing I was an immediate success, then made the mistake of asking myself, "What am I doing right?" whereupon I lost my balance and was dragged underwater. If during prayer you find yourself asking, "How am I doing?" answer, "Just fine," and return to your routine. As distractions intrude, just tell them "no" and let them float away like bubbles from champagne. Return to your routine of concentrated repetition tied to your breathing. Don't open your eyes to look at the clock. You are in no danger of falling asleep, and you will know accurately enough when to finish, even if it is longer or shorter than you intended. God is not timing you. Nothing matters but your passivity and attention.

Uptight people (of which I am one) find it difficult to relax sufficiently to make the most of contemplative prayer. If you are nervous, you will profit from mastering some simple techniques for calming yourself. *The Relaxation and Stress Reduction Workbook* by Dr. Martha Davis and collaborators (McKay, 1980) is a no-nonsense guide to many practical techniques for achieving the placid attention required for contemplation. Inexpensive audiotapes have helped me beat insomnia and lower my blood pressure. They can help a nervous person prepare for prayer. Available in bookstores (or through Potentials Unlimited, 4808-H Broadmoor SE, Grand Rapids, MI 49508), they rely on suggestion—a peaceful, persistent voice lulling you to a calm but attentive state. Using a tape may strike you as gimmicky, but it is preferable to nagging yourself to relax.

After some experience, many persons find it helpful to guide their own contemplative prayer by making an audiotape in their own voices. The obvious advantage of autosuggestion is that you can dispense with the preliminaries and listen from the outset, letting your voice on the tape talk you into a prayerful state. Here is what such a self-guided audiotape might say:

> *It's time again to be with you, God. I want to give you my total attention. I thank you for my life and my many blessings. I am sorry for all I have done to hurt myself and others, and for all the things I have left undone. Lord, it is easy to love you, but hard to love myself and others. Help me. You know better than I all the things I need. I know you will provide them. I know you will not demand of me more than I can do. Your grace is sufficient for me.*
>
> *Now I will stop talking, Lord, and let you speak. I will sit, eyes closed, hands loosely on my lap, breathing quietly, perfectly re-*

laxed and open to you. Despite my uncertainties and inadequacies, this is no time to worry about the past or future. I am at peace with myself because you love me and forgive me. You are always with me, but I am often unaware of your presence because I am preoccupied. For the next few minutes I will think only of you, and welcome you. I will let any distractions float away of their own accord. I love you, Lord; help me to pray.

Stop the tape and begin your prayer, synchronizing the same phrase to every inhalation and exhalation. If you are uncertain about making up your own prayer, you are safe with these ancient summonses:

> Come / Lord Jesus.
> *or*
> The Lord / is my shepherd.
> *or*
> Lord Jesus Christ / have mercy upon me, a sinner.

I would be derelict if I failed to refer you to a popular book, *The Relaxation Response* by Herbert Benson, M.D. (Avon, 1976), which offers evidence, from studies at Harvard Medical School and Boston's Beth Israel Hospital, of the extraordinary benefits to be derived from these techniques. However, I urge you to resist any temptation to enter into prayer for any reason short of allowing God to break through to you. Whatever the ancillary benefits of the regimen, you are not praying for your health but for the love of God. I pray that you will be patient long enough to be successful.

5

Cutting Through the Static

"Break on through to the other side!"

Jim Morrison of the Doors

The turbulent decade of the 1960s surprisingly produced a legacy of techniques that can assist you in developing your prayer life. The counterculture that lashed out at commercialism, militarism, and racial and sexual repression yielded only partial success politically, but it fostered new lifestyles. The flower children who stuffed bouquets down the barrels of rifles did not render those weapons less lethal, of course, but they succeeded in convincing their own generation that the violence and greed in human nature need to be suppressed. Hot is bad; cool is good.

Perhaps the lasting legacy of that innocent, violent decade is behavior modification, self-designed. Young people, now middle aged, purposely recreated themselves. They stopped smoking, took up transcendental meditation, yoga, karate, and tai chi. They joined encounter and self-awareness groups, formed ashrams and gathered in group houses, mingling the sexes and blurring the boundaries of gender. They started jogging and they cut their cholesterol intake. Their rock was not the church, of course; it was a musical idiom called rock. Some of them, like Jim Morrison, impatient for transformation, turned to drugs in a vain attempt to break through to the other side. They met death instead.

Doors of Perception

In his later years the pacifist author Aldous Huxley, an Englishman transplanted to Hollywood during the Second World War, became convinced that human behavior could be modified and humankind's aggressiveness stemmed. Although partially blind from an accident in his youth, Huxley undertook rigorous eye exercises and was successful enough to get a driver's license. Earlier, in his best-known novel, *Brave New World*, he had viciously satirized a futuristic world in which humanity would be kept pacified and satisfied by drugs. In the aftermath of the war's devastation, however, Huxley revised his thinking about the possible value of drugs in taming the human beast.

In a brief volume, *The Doors of Perception*, Huxley revealed his experience of ingesting mescaline, a natural hallucinogen used by Mexican Indians in religious rites, and exulted in its apparent ability to expand consciousness and calm the spirit. In his book *The Perennial Philosophy*, he had studied saints and ascetics who had achieved levels of consciousness in which they saw God (but with immense effort). Huxley now speculated that mind-bending drugs might be everyman's low-effort ticket to tame the violence of human nature and experience heaven on earth.

As it turned out, the drug culture yielded different results. Seeking cheap transcendence, a generation of dopesters burned out on cocaine, became more violent with crack, wasted away on heroin, lived nightmares on LSD, and mellowed out on marijuana at the expense of alertness and responsibility. But while hard drugs became the scourge of society, new prescription medications began to show remarkable success in behavior modification. Tranquilizers largely emptied our asylums. Manic depression and schizophrenia could now be treated. The drug Prozac is touted for turning human monsters into virtual pussycats. And although George Bush launched a nationwide war on drugs, the possibility of a kinder, gentler society may owe something to the availability of new prescription drugs that treat depression.

While the path to God is not through your medicine cabinet, there are nevertheless physical and mental *regimens* that can be utilized to improve your effectiveness in prayer. Unless you are a total couch potato, you already subscribe to one or more practical disciplines you believe are good for you. Diet, exercise, and grooming are tedious but fundamental; so too are education, hard work, and voluntarism. In combination these disciplines hold out the promise of a modicum of health, fitness, attractiveness, and longevity, along with a measure of self-respect. None of them, however, alone or in combination, promises the vision of God, which is the ultimate goal of prayer.

Prayer at the outset can be a tedious exercise, but it grows more successful and satisfying as it becomes habitual. Since you are *already* disciplined about other aspects of your life, the devotion you apply to your mind and body can be redirected to spiritual devotion. You are more prepared than you imagine to begin knocking on the doors of perception and having them opened to you. Thomas Merton, the young American poet turned Trappist monk, was knocking on the door when he uttered this prayer:

> O Lord God,
> I have no idea where I am going,
> I do not see the road ahead of me,
> I cannot know for certain where it will end.
> Nor do I really know myself,
> and the fact that I think
> I am following Your will
> does not mean that I am actually doing so.
> But I believe
> that the desire to please You
> does in fact please You.
> And I hope I have that desire
> in all that I am doing.

I hope that I will never do anything
apart from that desire to please You.
And I know that if I do this
You will lead me by the right road,
though I may know nothing about it.
Therefore I will trust you always
though I may seem to be lost
and in the shadow of death
I will not fear,
for you are ever with me,
and You will never leave me
to make my journey alone.

Meditation and Discipline

The man who does my office's publications told me that at the end of the day he likes nothing better than to stop at a quiet bar and linger over a drink, not to socialize exactly, but more to meditate—to sort out his day and clear his mind, reestablish priorities, and occasionally to ponder his fate. It is not heresy to prefer a quiet bar to a noisy church for meditation. I am fond of dropping by Saint John's across from the White House to think and pray, but often the organist is practicing or the cleaners are running the vacuum. Sunday church services are especially inappropriate occasions for meditation because they are designed for public worship, which is something different from private prayer.

My dependable quiet time is spent on my daily three-hour commutes between the nation's capital and exurban Virginia in a bus with forty fellow travelers. I pop in my earplugs; the white noise of the motor and air conditioner masks my neighbors' conversation. I do my thinking, my writing, and my praying on the bus.

That fact does not vouch for any extraordinary powers of concentration on my part—just that I have found a predictable time and place each day that works for me. You will need to find your own quiet time and place, because only you know your schedule. Many people pray before bedtime because it is the only regular time they can be sure will be free of preoccupation and anxiety. Theoretically you will find it harder to concentrate when you are exhausted at day's end. But practically speaking, it may be the one time you can relax sufficiently to follow the psalmist's counsel to "be still and know that I am God." Tiredness may be just the tranquilizer you need, and your regularity of prayer will serve as both a comfort and a discipline.

Opening the Doors of Perception

Our objective in prayer is to present God with our true selves and open ourselves to him. This dictates emptying ourselves of distraction, possessiveness, and egotism so that God can fill us with himself. Ironically, we must reach a certain level of self-confidence before we can let go of ourselves. Neurotics are notably handicapped in prayer. If you are down on yourself, you won't let God in.

Although strictly speaking they possess no religious significance in themselves, there are techniques and regimens that appear to provide the concentration and assurance that enhance the success of prayer. Yoga, the martial arts, and tai chi are Eastern disciplines that promote the integration of mind and body, producing both energy and calm. Contrast this with many people's experience of their bodies as shells they drag along like turtles. These disciplines, embraced in the proper spirit, not only are helpful on their own terms; they also prepare the ground for prayer by establishing calm, concentration, and openness, as well as integration of mind and body. Despite claims by cultists, however, these disciplines do not deliver arcane wisdom hidden from ordinary mortals, nor do they fully open the doors of perception. But they are among techniques that establish a grounding for prayer.

All three disciplines require training and persistence. Yoga, which calls for stretching postures, and the martial arts, which require energy, call for physical flexibility. They may be inappropriate for those who are older, handicapped, or in fragile health. Tai chi, which calls for measured and graceful movement, is probably more suitable for the elderly and frail but is equally effective for the young and fit. I have seen toddlers make the effort!

Mental Techniques

In addition to these active whole-body techniques, there are more passive disciplines that assist in inducing calm, clarity, confidence, and concentration. Besides expensive and lengthy psychotherapy, there are inexpensive generic aids you may find congenial, among them transcendental meditation, biofeedback, and hypnosis. You may already have tried one of these procedures in an effort to overcome a problem—something as mundane but critical as excess weight, a smoking habit, or insomnia.

Transcendental meditation (TM) was popularized in America in the sixties by a transplanted Indian monk, Maharishi Makesh Yogi, and was catapulted into a cult by its more fervent adherents. At heart, however, TM is only an ancient technique that induces deep relaxation, an inner calm and joy, and heightened ability to focus the mind and will. Simple as it seems, the technique rests on nothing more than concentrated attention and repetition of a word or meaningless sound during two twenty-minute periods in the course of a day, while you are comfortably seated in a quiet place with eyes closed. The maharishi gave his disciples their own mantras, customized Sanskrit words to repeat, but almost anything will do.

A colleague of mine swears by his daily exercise regimen, which helps him to find peace with his body as well as enhance his health. Serious runners who press themselves eventually experience what they call "runner's high," which may be the product of a release of endorphins—combination tranquilizers and pain suppressors produced naturally by the body. The high is not nervous excitement but rather an elation or feeling of well-being that can be placed at the service of prayer.

In her midteens, one of our daughters was plagued with anorexia. She and her body became enemies. Lisa was helped immensely by biofeedback, an electronic means of getting in touch with one's body with the object of establishing a modicum of control and friendship. The technique is not unlike a lie detector test or an electrocardiogram. Sensors monitor bodily tension and temperature. But where those other detectors move needles, biofeedback translates tension into sound: more tension equals higher pitch, less tension equals lower pitch. Listening to your body helps you to identify those idiosyncratic adjustments that calm it and produce the confidence that you are its controller, not its victim.

Hypnotism smacks of seduction but is demonstrably helpful for impressionable persons, of whom I am one. Rather than rely solely on willpower and gritty determination, you might consider hypnotic suggestion to help you to accomplish some difficult things that you want to do. The calm, persistent voice of the hypnotist somehow gets underneath superficial consciousness with repeated persuasion. Hypnotism has helped me conquer insomnia and control my blood pressure. Others employ it for confronting any number of harmful habits. If you know what you're after, you can probably dispense with a live hypnotist and rely instead on the subliminal audiotapes found in any large bookstore. You can even record your own suggestions on audiotape and listen to them with good results. If you go this route, what you are really seeking is the capability of *self* hypnosis or auto-suggestion—putting yourself in the calm, open, concentrated state that is conducive to prayer. The repeated recitation of a mantra or the Jesus Prayer probably rests on a similar mechanism to induce a prayerful attitude.

Being Practical

There is nothing magical, foolproof, or essential about these physical and mental techniques. If they help you to pray effectively, fine, but do not mistake a technique for prayer itself. Predictably, each technique has its fanatical followers, who magnify it into a kind of arcane secular religion. Do not be put off by them. Let yourself be helped by whatever works. Perhaps music puts you in the proper mood for prayer. Maybe your love for nature will help turn the key. All that matters is God and you. Remember that God's silence is only apparent and that your initiative provides him with an opening to speak to you. At the end of his autobiography, *The Seven Storey Mountain*, Thomas Merton concluded:

> Now my sorrow is over, and my joy is about to begin: the joy that rejoices in the deepest sorrows. For I am beginning to understand. You have taught me, and have consoled me, and I have begun again to hope and learn.
> I hear you saying to me:
> "I will give you what you desire. I will lead you into solitude. I will lead you by the way that you cannot possibly understand, because I want it to be the quickest way . . . And when you have been praised a little and loved a little I will take away all your gifts and all your love and all your praise and you will be utterly forgotten and abandoned and you will be nothing, a dead thing, a rejection . . . Do not ask when it will be or where it will be or how it will be . . . It does not matter. So do not ask me, because I am not going to tell you. You will not know until you are in it.
> "But you shall taste the true solitude of my anguish and my poverty and I shall lead you into the high places of my joy and you shall die in Me and find all things in My mercy which has created you for this end. . . .

This is undoubtedly more than you want God to say to you if

you are not called to a solitary life like Merton. But God will speak to your own situation. The important thing is to start praying and keep at it. Knock and the door will be opened.

My wife's godfather, Jeremy Levin, the CNN Beirut bureau chief who was taken hostage in Lebanon, read scripture in captivity and committed passages to memory. That's pretty standard practice for prayer, but it helped him to survive and to find God in more trying circumstances than you and I are ever likely to encounter. You will find your way. Keep in mind that no one else is keeping score (least of all God), so you shouldn't either. The object of prayer in any case is not prayer itself—it is God.

Merton advised, "If you want a life of prayer, the way to get it is by praying"; he added, "We already have everything, but we don't know it, and we don't experience it. Everything has been given to us . . . All we need do is experience what we already possess." As Saint Paul affirmed of the prayerful person, "He becomes a new person altogether—everything has become fresh and new" (2 Corinthians 5:17).

Centering in Prayer

Before we look in on those athletes of prayer, the mystics who have had a vision of God in this life, let me suggest a simple discipline that even they found helpful. Centering is not prayer itself but a kind of stretching exercise to prepare you for the effort. The ability we want to acquire is *centering*—letting go of self, blotting out noise and care, finding the calm and quiet that allows focused attention on God. There is no *doing* involved, but simply preparing an opening of self that God can fill.

This opening presumes that we have no grudges against God but fully trust in him. That is not obvious. God is the perfect Father, but your appreciation of him may be colored by your experience of your own father, who may have been less than completely trustworthy. But John Greenleaf Whittier felt confident in addressing God as our common Father:

> Dear Lord and Father of mankind,
> Forgive our foolish ways!
> Reclothe us in our rightful mind;
> In purer lives your service find,
> In deeper reverence, praise.
> Drop your still dews of quietness
> Till all our strivings cease:
> Take from our lives the strain and stress,
> And let our ordered lives confess
> The beauty of your peace.

Some believers abandon the practice of religion because of real or perceived mistreatment by parents, preachers, or others in authority. If your confidence is compromised by past experience, you will be seriously hampered in cultivating your relationship with God. You may need to talk seriously with someone *not* in authority who is comfortable with God to regain your courage and the confidence that God will not let you down. An odd statistic in American life is that more people pray than believe in God. That fact suggests that prayer is a natural impulse but that we can be put off by the way God is depicted to us by others. We *want* to pray, but not to *their* kind of God—a God of fear or sentimentality.

Too often people's fear of God is literal because of what they have been taught. For Christians, Jesus removed this fear and made God accessible by revealing (in Saint Paul's words)

> that sacred mystery which up till now has been hidden in every age and every generation, but which is now as clear as daylight to those who love God. They are those to whom God has planned to give a full vision of the full wonder and splendor of his secret plan for the sons of men. And the secret is simply this: Christ *in you!* Yes,

Christ *in you* bringing with him the hope of all the glorious things to come."

Colossians 1:26–27

Centering prayer possesses the virtue of simplicity and has been practiced successfully for at least seventeen centuries. It is based on the direct response to Jesus of Bartimaeus, the man he would cure of blindness (Mark 10:47), and on the prayer of the repentent official (Luke 18:13), whose sin Jesus declared forgiven. Their cries for mercy suggested the Jesus Prayer of the Desert Fathers, who sought through it to follow literally Saint Paul's instruction to pray without ceasing.

The basic formula of this prayer consists of nine words: "Lord Jesus Christ, have mercy on me, a sinner." These words are matched to your regular breathing: (*inhale*) "Lord Jesus Christ" (*exhale*) "have mercy on me, a sinner." The object is to render prayer as natural as breathing. Some shorten the prayer to a repetition of the one word "Jesus" as a mantra, tied to the rhythm of breathing. The advantage of centering prayer over other kinds of meditation is that it gives the mind something to do and thereby serves to shrug off distractions. Unlike most mantras, the Jesus Prayer has meaning. But in contrast to discursive prayer, the mantra in centering prayer does not require analysis and dissection to be understood. And unlike prayers that address God from a distance, the Jesus Prayer is intimate and personal.

It is also democratic and accessible. When your prayer becomes as simple as breathing, you will not be tempted to compare it with the prayers of others. Centering prayer does not derive its benefit from one's intelligence, sophistication, or desperation. Christians believe it works precisely because God's Spirit enables us to enter Jesus' own prayer to his Father. When I drive my car, I do not analyze the workings of the pistons, valves, and transmission, but simply step on the gas and steer. So with prayer. God makes it work.

Now let us turn from basic prayer to the most advanced—to the prayers of those who have touched the face of God.

Mysticism

On his deathbed Saint Thomas Aquinas dismissed the accumulated wisdom of his extraordinary lifetime as mere "straw." For that extraordinary man there was a treasure to discard. In the multiple volumes of his *Summa Theologica,* the thirteenth-century friar had produced an exhaustive synthesis of reason and revelation unequaled in the seven centuries since his death—a tightly reasoned and unsentimental compendium of all we can expect to understand about God this side of the grave. In the end, however, Aquinas found something simpler and better—a direct personal experience of God. The ultimate man of reason had become a mystic.

Saint Paul acknowledged that "at present we are men looking at puzzling reflections in a mirror," but he promised, "The time will come when we shall see reality whole and face to face. At present all I know is a little fraction of the truth, but the time will come when I shall know it as fully as God now knows me!" (1 Corinthians 13:12). But what if a direct and undistorted experience is possible while you and I still inhabit this mortal coil? Surely reading and hearing *about* God and praying *to* him are inferior to confronting him face-to-face. Not to put too fine a point on it, it would be the difference between writing love letters and making love. Why bother courting God if we can possess him?

We are still in a century-long reaction against the excesses of Romanticism, which celebrated sensation but was dissatisfied with the senses, yearning instead for a transcendence mystics identify with union with God. The music of the Austrian post-Romantic composer Gustav Mahler poignantly reveals this yearning. Not leaving music alone to express his quest, Mahler incorporated texts of poets. Here are the final lines of Hans

Bethge for "The Parting" in Mahler's *Das Lied von der Erde*
(The Song of the Earth), straining for eternity:

> I shall return to my homeland, to my home!
> Never again to wander so far.
> My heart rests in expectation of its hour:
> Forever this lovely earth will flower anew as in spring!
> Everywhere and always the horizon will be blue!
> Forever . . . forever.

The Problem with Pantheism

Let's be clear at the outset about what the mystic seeks—not
the comradeship the apostles enjoyed in daily life with Jesus,
but an ecstatic, all-absorbing experience of the Godhead. Nor
does Christianity have an monopoly on mysticism. The mystic
quest predates the Christian era and survives in religious traditions with quite different notions of God, notably in faiths that
place a high value on meditation. Mysticism, in fact, thrives
with a *pantheistic* view of the universe, in which all creation is
conceived not only as infused with spirit, reflecting God, but
also as *inseparable* from God and identified with him. For the
pantheist, all that is is God. The creature cannot be separated
from its creator, and any apparent distinction of this-versus-
that or "I"-versus-"Thou" is illusory.

In this respect the generic mystic is not unlike Henry David
Thoreau, who aimed at becoming "one with nature." The spiritual seeker takes the search one more giant step and identifies
nature with God. Regrettably, Christian mystics tend to employ the same inadequate language as pantheists to describe
their experience of God, but they are careful to retain the distinction between creature and creator. In the mystic union,
Christians are swept up—but not swallowed up—by God.
Rather, they retain their own heightened identity.

If a direct knowledge of God is possible, why bother with improving our prayer life? Because the experience is rare and un-predictable and invariably assumes a long facility with prayer and meditation. A prayerful life consists of knocking on God's door (Matthew 7:7–8). Although the final door of perception will surely be opened to us on the other side of the grave, it is (alas) only rarely opened on this side.

Not surprisingly, the mystical experience of God during one's earthly sojourn is a gift fraught with difficulty. It is not at all like a day in Disneyland but can be preceded by deep de-pression and the sense of isolation and abandonment that Saint John of the Cross termed the "dark night of the soul." Like all deep romances, it can be tempestuous and heart-wrenching. Many devout believers have never experienced an emotional conversion but have followed the same faith since childhood with no emotional props or special revelations. So, too, only a minute fraction of the faithful expect the mystical experience of direct knowledge of God in this life, which is a demanding passion—a love affair that leaves room for little else. What you and I and the vast majority of believers who are not mystics possess of our God is neither second rate nor even secondhand. Christians, Jews, and Moslems all inherit God's revelation and his abiding love, which are sufficient to last them—and you—until we all join God for eternity.

Reporting from the Scene

In the world of journalism, where I have made my living, noth-ing takes the place of eyewitness news—reporting from the scene. Yet even the journalist on the spot is not a participant but a spectator. By contrast, the mystic is a unique participant in the ultimate adventure. Even if we don't share that experi-ence, you and I can learn from it. To give them their due, mys-tics take pains to explain the inexpressible. Since we will *all* be mystics in the next life, it is worth noting what these unusual people have to say about God and about life.

"Fire . . . the God of Abraham, Isaac and Jacob, not the God of the philosophers . . . Certainty, Certainty, emotion, joy, peace, the God of Jesus Christ. Thy God shall be my God. Oblivion of the world and of everything except God. Joy, Joy, Joy, tears of Joy!" This account by the French philosopher and mathematician Blaise Pascal describes an experience following his meditation on Peter's denial of Jesus. A personal crisis had brought home to Pascal his own desolate separation from God and his pardon through Jesus. Pascal blamed himself for the separation and imposed penances on himself, wearing a hair shirt and resting on a bed of nails. Remarkably, his extraordinary vision was never revealed by him during his lifetime. After his death a written account was found sewn into his clothing. He had literally *worn* the experience to the end of his life on earth.

I confess that in my youth, fascinated by Somerset Maugham's *The Razor's Edge,* I naively aspired to such ecstatic experiences, which I then assumed were confined to Eastern religion. As I got older and learned of the cost to mystics of such experiences, I became content with much less, on the principle that one does not have to be a hero to believe in heroism. Rather, my ordinary faith is strengthened by these extraordinary believers.

The Via Negativa

Mystical experience is a gift from God, the revelation of a journey few Christians will choose to take. But for those of us who struggle with faith in everyday life, it is stunning to read the reports of those who have taken the path of prayer to its end and have reached its object—God. While the yellow brick road of Oz led to a wizard who was a sham, the path of prayer leads to fulfillment.

Mystics in Eastern faiths tend to regard the material world as evil and seek escape from it. By contrast, mystics in the Judeo-

Christian-Islamic tradition honor the material world as God's creation—hence good—but nevertheless distracting. Accordingly, they follow the *via negativa*, a path to God that shuns materiality without denigrating it. Their prayer journeys are not unlike travel through the emptiness of space or the darkness of a forest at night. They use terms such as "desert," "wilderness," or "the cloud of unknowing" to describe the extremes to which they are willing to be stripped of ego and attachments so God can fill them.

In his *Five Songs After Poems by Friedrich Ruckert,* Gustav Mahler portrayed the dark night literally, as midnight:

> At midnight
> my mind traveled
> beyond dark borders.
> No hint of light
> could console me . . .
> At midnight
> I yielded all my power
> into your hands, Lord.
> Over death and life
> you stand guard, a sentinel
> at midnight.

By and large, Christian mystics favor focusing on the "hidden God" or "wholly Other" rather than on Jesus as incarnate mediator. Consequently, their connection with God often presents the appearance of not being mediated at all but of being direct. Over the centuries this preference has opened them to criticism for giving Christ short shrift.

Christians assume that Jesus had such experiences. At the transfiguration, three apostles witnessed Jesus caught up in a blinding light and conversing with the prophets. Stephen in his martyrdom saw Jesus enthroned, and Paul mentions mystical experiences of his own that were centered on Christ.

Mysticism thrived in the late Middle Ages at a time of plague and political upheaval in Europe, when theology was becoming mannered, lauding reason and logic over sentiment and emotion. In reaction many Christians turned to penance, self-denial, and prayer to seek out God in a harsh, insensitive world. Richard Rolle, an English hermit, spoke of his intimacy with God as rapture, fire, sweetness, and song. The unknown author of *The Cloud of Unknowing* (c. 1370) claimed that love, not reason and revelation, was the key to union with God. The English mystic Walter Hilton claimed in *The Scale of Perfection* that contemplation could achieve a "soft, sweet, burning love" so that "the soul for the time being becomes one with God and is conformed to the image of the Trinity."

Censure and Success

Not unexpectedly, the church censured many mystics as presumptuous, vague, and unhelpful to the majority of believers—and occasionally heretical. The notion that one might go to God directly rather than through the church did not sit well with the religious bureaucracy. But there were mystics whose stature even the most hostile churchmen could not impugn. My personal favorites happened to be close friends and saints: the sixteenth-century Spaniards Teresa of Avila and John of the Cross. Teresa, well born, vivacious, and social, became increasingly aware of the shallowness of her inner life. At the age of forty she began to experience ecstatic visions that led to what she called her "second conversion." Unusually articulate for a mystic, Teresa charted the stages of prayer leading to the vision of God. They were discursive prayer, emotional recollection, the presence of God in quiet, and finally union, or "marriage."

Despite the mystics' reliance on romantic language, it will not do to dismiss mystical experience out of hand as a sexual substitute for celibate men and women, any more than to claim that love in anyone's life is just sex. Although human discourse is sometimes equivocal, the inherent limitations of lan-

guage did not dissuade God from revealing himself in the
Bible in words we can understand. We know enough about
God's love to realize what it does for us and what it calls forth
in response.

John of the Cross covered a somewhat bleaker landscape
than Teresa in his journey to God, but it was every bit as successful. By his account the traveler first enters the "dark night
of the senses" by renouncing pride and greed, then moves to
the "dark night of the soul," feeling unanchored and alienated,
abandoned by God and incapable of prayer. What is really accomplished at this stage, according to John, is total surrender
of the self and abandonment to God, following which one is
"betrothed" and "illuminated," prepared for union with God.

John Wesley's conversion experience, by contrast, seems
tame but was just as revolutionary. An Anglican priest, Wesley
was ineffective in his early ministry in England and colonial
America. But in 1738, while listening to a reading of Luther's
commentary on the epistle to the Romans, he experienced a
vision of Jesus and a conviction that Christ had died to save
him. His heart, Wesley wrote, "was strangely warmed," and he
lived throughout his life carrying the same conviction (if not
the same experience) to others.

Protestant mystics added to the vocabulary of the experience in a way that was consistent with their individualism, em-
phasizing the divine element in man: a "spark," "center," or
"ground"—the "holy self" or "the Christ within." Protestant individualism predictably regarded institutional settings as su-
perfluous to prayer. Thus the eighteenth-century English
divine William Law insisted: "The one true way of dying to self
wants no cells, no monasteries or pilgrimages. It is the way of
patience, humility and resignation to God."

Every morning I turn to the sports section of *The Washington
Post* to see how my heroes are faring. Far from being intimi-
dated or discouraged that they (and not I) can bat four hundred, serve and volley, race an open car at two hundred miles
per hour, plunge for one hundred yards on the AstroTurf, or

execute layups with ballet precision, I exult in what they can do. And it is not simply vicarious experience. Because they can do it, *I know it can be done.*

So also it is with prayer and the sole objective you and I have in common with every man, woman, and child past, present, and to come. Others have broken through to the other side, or, more precisely, have allowed God to break into their lives. The effort takes much practice and not a little passion. Thus William Blake could exclaim:

> Bring me my bow of burning gold;
> Bring me my arrows of desire . . .
> I will not cease from mental fight,
> Nor shall my sword sleep in my hand
> Till we have built Jerusalem . . . "

6

The Best Prayer and the Best Pray-er

※

"Lord, teach us to pray, as John used to teach his disciples."

Luke 11:1

The greeting card industry in the United States makes millions of dollars each year compensating for our inability to express ourselves to people we care about.

"How do I love thee? Let me count the ways..." Why should I attempt the composition of a personal love letter when Elizabeth Barrett Browning has already done it better and is no longer around to object to my borrowing her words? I do not mind leaning on the anonymous authors who compose greetings for Hallmark and Ambassador to express how you and I feel about weddings, anniversaries, births, illness, death, graduation, promotion—about our mothers, fathers, children, and secretaries, and about Christmas, Easter, and even Saint Patrick's Day.

Offer a professor of English literature a choice in sending birthday greetings to a young child, and the choice is automatic: not an original composition, but a card featuring Peanuts or Garfield. Our lack of courage in expressing our

104

sentiments is in sharp contrast with the previous century, when Richard Wagner could toss off the *Siegfried Idyll* to honor the birth of his son, and Claude Debussy could compose the *Children's Corner* Suite to amuse his young child. Walking through an eighteenth-century cemetery not far from my home, I am always struck by the inscriptions on the tombstones of persons long gone. Here etched in worn stone are the brief but poignant profiles of devoted mothers, faithful fathers, loving children, and generous citizens. People then were not afraid to express themselves.

When our own children were small we spent our annual vacations in homes exchanged with other families. One summer, on a vacation to Connecticut, we came upon an heirloom of our host family—a register from the nineteenth century signed by relatives, guests, and neighbors over many years. The album was filled with penned appreciations by adults and children, sweetly and (I suspect) honestly expressing the value they placed on love, friendship, and gratitude. All were sentiments written by very ordinary people, but by today's greeting card standards, they were in a class with Elizabeth Barrett Browning.

Improvization in Prayer

Nevertheless, I do not altogether regret that this year I will choose a greeting card and sentiment for my wife's birthday identical to that selected by tens of thousands of other American husbands. It is a reminder to me that I am neither the center of the universe nor the world's greatest lover. The planets do not make their heavenly orbits around me or my marriage. Were I to summon the courage to write my wife a love letter in lieu of sending a commercial card, the product would in any event bear a close resemblance to the efforts of other uxorious American males in advanced middle age.

The pioneering photographer Ernst Haas, who looked at

life through a camera, concluded: "Each man on earth is nothing but a mosaic of a picture he will never see." I am but a piece
of a big picture, and my thoughts and sentiments, while they
are indeed mine, are not unique. Viewed from that perspective, the improvisation of emotion is pretentious. Formulas, by
contrast, offer some dependability. Martin Marty, the articulate American Lutheran theologian, acknowledged to writer
Jim Castelli that he is not at all adept at improvised prayer:

> Meditation doesn't do it for me. What I do therefore—it's
> kind of a crass-sounding term—is "hitchhike." I hitchhike
> using the vehicles, the instruments of people who are bet-
> ter at devotion than I am. I'm not someone who could
> write like Mozart or who could play Mozart, but I am en-
> nobled when I listen to Mozart or read his scores. I'm not
> a prayerful genius like the religious philosopher and sci-
> entist Pascal. I am not even someone who could edit and
> expound Pascal. But I can read him prayerfully, and the
> thoughts he inspires will convey me to different levels of
> being, to new depths. So I spend a lot of time with an-
> thologies of prayer, with quotations, sourcebooks . . . and
> so on. Whether all those trips produce the language of "I"
> and "Thou" I'm not sure, but I am a book person, and
> therefore if I draw close to God, it is likely to be through
> reading.

Prayer is a love letter to God. It is not easy to compose, just as
it is not easy to love. Love "at first sight" is rare and suspect.
Love takes learning; devotion takes practice. One might imagine that the twelve men who lived closest to Jesus day by day in
his adult life would have found it easy to express themselves to
him. The gospels confirm the contrary. Jesus' friends were, if
anything, even more tongue-tied emotionally than you and I.
But they didn't fake a facility they lacked. They asked Jesus,
"Teach us to pray." And he complied.

Here is Jesus' familiar response in its less familiar J. B.
Phillips translation:

Our Heavenly Father, may your name be honoured;
May your kingdom come, and your will be done on earth as it
is in Heaven.
Give us this day the bread we need,
Forgive us what we owe to you, as we have also forgiven those
who owe anything to us.
Keep us clear of temptation, and save us from evil.

If you come from a Christian background, you probably
have the Lord's Prayer committed to memory in a standard,
ritual translation. Encoded in your gray matter, it rests waiting
to be summoned as automatically (and as mindlessly) as the
Pledge of Allegiance to the flag and the first verse of our National Anthem. In ritual, religious or secular, familiarity does
not necessarily breed contempt, but it can numb our sense of
the words. The Lord's Prayer, although it is ancient, is not at all
quaint: It is practical, comprehensive, and contemporary. It
bears analysis to restore the meaning the apostles would have
found in it as the answer to their question: how are we to pray?
You do not have to be a Christian to make this prayer your
own, but you must enter the valley of prayer, where familiar
words retain the force of their meaning. In his many folk per-
formances over the years, the blind balladeer Doc Watson has
sung this call to prayer that he learned from his mother:

> As I went down to the valley to pray
> Studying about the good old way:
> Who shall wear the robe and crown?
> Good Lord, show me the way.

This is precisely the purpose of the Lord's Prayer.

The Context of Prayer

The Lord's Prayer consists of verses 9 to 13 of the sixth chapter
of Saint Matthew's gospel. While the prayer stands by itself, it

emerges from an extensive context as part of what has come to be known as the Sermon on the Mount. Jesus introduced the prayer this way:

> When you pray, don't be like play-actors. They love to stand and pray in the synagogues and at street corners so people may see them at it. Believe me, they have had all the reward they are going to get. But when you pray, go into your own room, shut your door and pray to your Father privately. Your Father who sees all private things will reward you. And when you pray don't rattle off long prayers like the pagans who think they will be heard because they use so many words. Don't be like them. After all, God, who is your Father, knows your needs before you ask him.
>
> *Matthew 6:5–8*

Jesus footnotes the Lord's Prayer when he adds: "if you forgive other people their failures, your Heavenly Father will also forgive you. But if you will not forgive other people, neither will your Heavenly Father forgive you your failures" (Matthew 6:14–15).

Unfortunately, the very familiarity of Jesus' brief prayer is an impediment to its usefulness. Let us then revisit its key phrases.

"Our Father"

Jesus invites us to address God as he does—as a loving parent. Not simply as creator or director, but as a *relative*—everyone's Father. This redefines religion. Despite paganism's predilection to personify its deities, its faith never came close to depicting God in terms of a loving, caring relationship with every man, woman, and child.

Jesus is preeminently God's Son, but we are also God's sons and daughters by adoption—and Jesus' brothers and sisters in the flesh. Moreover, we are made in God's image, somehow partaking of God's nature. While Jesus alone can affirm that "the Father and I are one," he summons you and me to "be perfect, as my heavenly father is perfect." Jesus could not offer such an invitation were we not also his Father's children.

When I was writing *Growing in Faith,* I was cautioned by a friend who is a seminary president to make the references in my text gender neutral; that is, whenever possible to choose "humanity" or "humankind" over "mankind," to employ "one" rather than "him" when referring to an individual who could be either a woman or a man, and to stress God's parenthood rather than God's fatherhood. This reconstruction of language is not as easy as it sounds and, even when successful, makes for awkward reading. Moreover, when taken too literally, gender correctness distorts reality.

It is perfectly true that God is *above* gender—that the parental relationship is more important than strict *father*hood. It is understandable when a feminist priest or minister slips in a reference to God as our *Mother* just to shake up our stodgy preconceptions. But God, while he neither wears trousers nor sports a beard, is clearly not our heavenly mother, and we run the serious risk of depersonalizing God altogether if we insist on degenderizing him. It is no insult to women that Jesus had a human mother and a divine father, nor indeed that Jesus was a man rather than a woman. To tinker with the facts in the interests of feminizing God would result in an absurdity—Jesus' having two mothers and no father. Christians celebrate both Mother's Day and Father's Day. The extraordinary devotion of Christian men and women to Jesus' mother through the centuries, while considered excessive by many theologians, is a tribute to his human parent, whom he needed as much as his Father.

We cannot be insensitive to the fact that, on occasion, institutional church leaders have appropriated the "gender" of the

Father, Jesus, and the apostles as an excuse to impede women's access to the ministry, but that is altogether another problem Christianity must deal with. It cannot be solved by altering the character of the Father and Son.

The fatherhood of God, while stressed by Jesus, is consistent in the history of Judaism. In the story of the Exodus from Egypt, God instructed Moses to tell Pharoah, "This is what Yahweh says: 'Israel is my first-born son'" (Exodus 4:22). The prophet Hosea expressed the tenderness of the parental relationship: "When Israel was a child I loved him, and out of Egypt I called my son . . . it was I who taught Ephraim to walk, I took [my people] in my arms . . . and I bent down to them and fed them" (Hosea 11:1, 3–4).

God's parenthood is so all-embracing that Jesus, in hyperbole, warns us against comparing any merely human relationship to it: "And don't call any human being 'father'—for you have one Father and he is in heaven" (Matthew 23:9). Saint Paul underscores the fact: "It is because you really are his sons that God has sent the Spirit of his Son into your hearts to cry 'Father, dear Father.' You, my brother, are not a servant any longer; you are a son. And, if you are a son, then you are certainly an heir of God through Christ" (Galatians 4:6–7).

The Lord's Prayer was composed by Jesus to be said in the company of others. It addresses God as *"our* Father," not as exclusively *"my* Father." You and I share him with everyone else, alive, deceased, or yet to be born. God possesses us; we do not in any sense have exclusive rights to him. It is in the nature of siblings to compete for parental affection, but God does not play favorites. As we know from Jesus' parables, the stray sheep and the prodigal son are as precious to God as a faithful son and daughter. Christianity is a radically democratic religion, with equal rights and privileges for all—as coheirs with Jesus of an eternal glory in which we shall amazingly "share in God's essential nature" (2 Peter 1:4).

Here is the grateful gloss on the Lord's Prayer of the American theologian Reinhold Niebuhr, addressed to the one Father we all share:

We thank you, our Father, for the provisions made for the needs of the bodies and souls of men, for the ordered course of nature and for the miracle of the harvest by which our life is sustained. Teach us to distribute to all according to their need what you have intended for their sustenance. We thank you for our physical life, with its strength and gladness, and for the glimpses of the eternal which shine through human joys and woes. We praise you for the human mind and its power to survey the world in its length and breadth, and for the infinities of thought and truth which carry our imagination beyond our comprehension. We thank you, too, that the world which exceeds our comprehension is not lost in mystery, but that through seers and saints, and finally Jesus Christ, we have been given light upon the meaning of the mystery which surrounds you. Grant us grace to walk in humility and gratitude before you.

"Who are in heaven"

Because we believe that God knows and sees everything, we assume he must have a vantage point to view his universe, as the Greek gods had on Mount Olympus. "God is watching," we tell a mischievous child. None of us really believes in a three-tiered universe (heaven "up there," hell "down there," and us in the middle), but this myth from childhood dies hard. What can we replace it with?

A millennium before Jesus walked the earth, King Solomon affirmed that "the heavens and their own heavens cannot contain God" (1 Kings 8:27). The psalmist agreed: "If I climb up into heaven, thou art there; if I go down to hell, thou art there also. If I take the wings of the morning, and remain in the uttermost parts of the sea; even there also shall thy hand lead me, and thy right hand shall hold me." (Psalm 139: 8–10).

Although God is everywhere, he is not just coextensive with his own universe, because that would give him dimensions.

Heaven is clearly not a *place* at all, but a perfection. The late English Jesuit Thomas Corbishley suggested that we are better off rendering "heavenly" as "unearthly." The perfection of God is everything we are not. He is immaterial, not spread across space but wholly present in every place.

The poet Robert Browning was mocked for proclaiming that "God's in his heaven, all's right with the world." His critics recognized rightly that the world wants for perfection, and so do we. But to give the poet his due, Browning was referring to providence. He knew that God is capable of making our crooked paths straight even when we cannot.

If heaven is literally inconceivable, nevertheless God's kingdom is palpable for the man and woman of faith. The Spirit of God already makes his home in our individual hearts, minds, and bodies, where he strains to realize the kingdom within us. So look for God not in some distant heaven but in your inner kingdom.

"Hallowed be thy name"

Why hallow God's *name* when we ought to praise God for himself? That is certainly our contemporary fashion in thinking, but the Lord's Prayer reflects ancient ways. While you and I think of names only as convenient but arbitrary labels for things that allow us to share information about the world we live in, the ancients endowed words with a significance that gave them an almost independent reality.

In his gospel, Saint John refers to God's Son as the Word uttered by God from all eternity, which became incarnate in Jesus: "So the word of God became a human being and lived among us." In the Old Testament, God changes Abram's name to Abraham, signifying that he is now "the father of nations." Likewise Jesus renames Simon the apostle Peter, the "rock" on which he will build his church.

There is power in naming things. Scientists name stars and

elements for their own kind; explorers and politicians name whole nations for themselves. We name our children and our pets. (One of our cats is named for the Roman, Brutus, another for the Queen of Sheba.) In the Genesis story, the first man and woman assert their dominion over all the creatures in Eden by giving them names.

Lofty personages take their names seriously. Elizabeth II will always be compared to Elizabeth I because she bears the same name. A guard at the Tower of London corrected my wife when she asked a question about "Elizabeth the Great." He replied testily, "Our present queen is also great." When another queen, Victoria, pronounced, "*We* are not amused," she was referring to herself not as an individual like you or me, but as an institution. This reminds me of Richard Nixon, who in later years referred to his past prominence in the third person: "When Nixon was president of the United States and leader of the free world . . . " In each instance the careful use of names by individuals both exalts and protects their persons.

In sharp contrast, God has told us his name: Yahweh—*I am who am.* In deference to the diety, however, Judaism makes every effort *not* to address God by his proper name but rather to use substitutes such as "Lord" or "Holy One." If you are like me, you resent total strangers presuming to call you by your first name until you become better acquainted and give permission for familiarity. To hallow God's *name* is to affirm that he is holy, set apart, sacred, and unique. It is unwise to get too cozy with God; we are not exactly in his league.

As a journalist I find use of the passive voice anathema even in prayer, and I avoid it at any cost if possible. However, to rewrite Jesus' prayer in the active voice, we would have to say "*We* hallow your name." But then, as C. S. Lewis suggests, you and I would be pretending that we mortals are the only ones praising God, whereas in fact we are joined by countless angels and all creation in a chorus of praise.

"Thy kingdom come"

That is, may God's reign, with its beauty and peace, extend over our lives *here*, in our hearts and in all the places we inhabit. In an age accustomed to democracy, we think of government in terms of elective politics, which is a conflict of counterbalancing forces. In the past, however, a good king could concentrate his time not on campaigning and competing for votes but on securing peace and prosperity. That is what we have in mind in God's kingdom.

I am reminded of Edward Hicks's painting *The Peaceable Kingdom*, in which the lion is lying down with the lamb and is less threatening than a tabby cat. Hicks's recreation of Eden may be fanciful, but peace is a social and personal reality—not simply the absence of turmoil but the fulfillment of our natures.

Let us not forget to pray also for the dead, that God's kingdom may also come to them. When loved ones die we sensibly pray that they may have a "perfect rest"—not that they be cocooned for eternity, but that they become citizens of God's peaceable kingdom.

Father Corbishley recalled instances in the Old Testament where men attributed a harshness to God that masked their own responsibilities to confirm the kingdom. For example, claiming that God "hardened Pharaoh's heart" (Exodus 4:21; 7:3) to persecute the Jews makes God the heavy, whereas Pharaoh needed no encouragement whatsoever in his tyranny. If God is not a democrat, neither is he a tyrant. His kingdom is altruistic, peaceable, loving, and compassionate.

But what are we to make of Jesus' claim that the kingdom is already here? Why pray for what we already possess? Because only the seeds of the kingdom are in our hearts. *People* have been redeemed, not society. Politics is our work: with the urging of the Spirit within, to affirm and realize the kingdom of God among all God's creatures.

"Thy will be done"

C. S. Lewis cautions us not to simply submit passively to God's wishes, nor to assume that God's will for us is replete with trials and disappointments to be endured. It is insulting to God's graciousness just to hunker down for life's inevitable disappointments, thanking him only for the occasional blessing. God's will for us is much more generous than we imagine. In the Third World's developing nations, formerly subject peoples possess what political scientists term "rising expectations." They recognize that their quality of life can be improved and are willing to work for it. We can learn a lesson from them. In the long run what we are requesting is that God give us "the same mind that was also in Christ"—to take on the motivation of the one person who always followed God's will. "My food is doing the will of him who sent me and finishing the work he has given me" (John 4:34). Jesus' obedience to God's will brought about our redemption. By imitating him we collaborate in the full realization of the kingdom.

Brother Ramon, a contemporary Anglican lay hermit, prays for God's will in this poignant way:

> Have your own way, Lord, have your own way,
> You are the potter, I am the clay;
> Mould me and make me after your will,
> As I am waiting, yielded and still.

"On earth as it is in heaven"

What would a kingdom be like where God's will is done? Here is Scripture's attempt to depict the new heaven and new earth: "Violence will no longer be heard of in your country, nor devastation and ruin within your frontiers . . . No more will the sun give daylight, nor moonlight shine upon you, but Yahweh will be your everlasting light. Your God will be your splendor" (Isaiah 60: 18–19). Saint John exults:

See! The home of God is with men, and he will live among them. They shall be his people, and God himself shall be with them, and will wipe away every tear from their eyes. Death shall be no more, and never again shall there be sorrow or crying or pain . . . See! I am making all things new . . . I will give to the thirsty water without price from the fountain of life . . . The city has no need for the light of sun or moon, for the splendor of God fills it with light and its radiance is the Lamb.

Revelation 21: 3–6, 23

If this apocalyptic description falls short of satisfying us, it at least suggests that the kingdom is a surprise and certainly not a bore.

"Give us this day our daily bread"

Jesus' redundancy here is significant. The faithful believer is not a hoarder, stockpiling necessities against a rainy day, like some 1950s householder provisioning his bomb shelter against a nuclear holocaust. Rather, he asks God today for what is sufficient to get him through the day. Remember that the Lord's Prayer emerges from the Sermon on the Mount, where Jesus speaks of the lilies of the field. He is telling us not to be greedy out of anxiety for tomorrow.

Recovering alcoholics live by the rule "One day at a time," realizing that this is the best they can manage in the trial to remain sober. All of us are brought up to believe that we must secure our futures today by planning for tomorrow's every contingency. All my insurance policies are contrivances to cushion me from future disaster. Of course, God is our ultimate insurance policy. He also supplies our present needs, which are really the only ones we have, because we have no alternative but to live in the present.

To ask for today's necessities *today* puts a realistic edge on our prayer. Once we get started, we will be tempted to meander in our devotions and to seek God's help with our psyches, our jobs, our appearance, our love life, and other, cosmic, long-range concerns. Prayer can easily become dreamy and speculative when it takes on the big picture. Better we admit that we are hungry now and depend on God for today's rations.

Fortunately, practical devotion need not reflect desperation. We will not be surprised if the prayer of a soldier going into battle is panicky, but when we ask for "our daily bread," we are only admitting our persistent dependency. Our lives are not on the line. If at day's end we happen to go to bed hungry, we will still be alive tomorrow to renew our prayer.

Two final observations: (1) When I am hungry it is a solitary need; I do not feel the hunger of others. Yet Jesus tells individuals to pray for *our* daily bread—to satisfy our common necessities. (2) Jesus also said that man does not live by bread alone, so there are other acute needs we may have of which we are unaware. I have walked around with pneumonia and other infections for weeks before a doctor happened to discover the maladies. You may think you need a new job or a new spouse when you really need a vacation or an extra hour of sleep each night. This wisdom is part of the "daily bread" we pray for.

"Forgive us our trespasses as we forgive those who trespass against us"

This is the nub of it—the hardest thing to do, yet the most reasonable. How can we expect God to forgive us if we do not forgive others?

But how it goes against the grain! And how we avoid getting into situations where we might have an enemy to forgive! Ever since you and I graduated from a childhood in which disputes were settled by fists, we have inhabited a world of adults who studiously avoid confrontation. This avoidance of antagonizing people we dislike is less a reflection of kindliness than our realization that should we make an enemy of someone, we must then either sustain our hostility or forgive him. Neither is an appetizing alternative.

Oddly, God appears to demand more of us in this respect than he does of himself. He forgives us on condition that we repent of our offenses and failings, but he expects us to forgive enemies who are not at all repentant themselves or may be oblivious to the harm they have caused us. More often than not, they have no interest in our forgiveness and may even disdain it.

I suspect that is the key. By forgiving we are letting go of enmity, which festers in us. When we nurture hatred we burden ourselves, becoming in that sense our own enemies. When Jesus forgave his executioners from the cross, they took no notice. But the act of forgiveness liberated Jesus to cry, "Father, I commend my spirit into your hands," uncompromised and fully at peace with the world he thereby redeemed.

Recovering alcoholics in one of their hardest steps toward sobriety must personally apologize to everyone they harmed in their years under the influence. What possible good can apologies accomplish after the harm is done and long past? Old loves and friendships often cannot be restored. Yet in the act of asking and giving forgiveness, addicts find a palpable weight lifted from their lives and a modicum of peace restored. By forgiving others we manage to "forgive" ourselves.

Early in the century just ending, the French aristocrat Charles de Foucauld returned to the Sahara, where he had served as a cavalry officer; he came this time not as a warrior but as a solitary determined to emulate Jesus' own prayerful life in the desert. Foucauld was murdered by tribesmen jealous of his moral influence, but the hermit knew what it meant to forgive and to seek forgiveness:

I say, "Father, forgive me." With my whole soul I see how horrible are my sins to you, how they disgust and insult you, and what a price your Son had to pay to redeem me from them. I realize how much pain I have caused you; and in that realization I feel pain myself, crying with remorse at what I have done. At the same time I recognize that I have no right to ask your forgiveness for my sins unless I forgive others their sins. And, of course, the sins which others commit against me are nothing compared with the sins I have committed against you. Thus in truth I am asking that all mankind might be forgiven.

"Lead us not into temptation, but deliver us from evil"

This is yet another of those ancient expressions intended to ascribe all power to God but that leave the impression that God might actually choose to place us in harm's way. Instead, we are asking that he protect us from situations in which we might be harmed or tempted to harm others. Ultimately, we are responsible for ourselves; that is the blessing (as well as the price) of being free. Life is full of trials and tests. At one point Saint Paul asked to be relieved of one of them—"a thorn in his flesh," he called it. But God answered him by leaving the thorn there: "My grace is enough for you: for where there is weakness, my power is shown the more completely" (2 Corinthians 12:7–9). This led Paul to reassure the Corinthians, from his own experience:

> No temptation has come your way that is too hard for flesh and blood to bear. But God can be trusted not to allow you to suffer any temptation beyond your powers of endurance. He will see to it that every temptation has a way out, so that it will never be impossible for you to bear it.
>
> *1 Corinthians 10:13*

For the prayerful believer, the "strength that comes from weakness" is steadfastness in humility. Lacking faith, the world regards Christ on his cross as a loser. But in faith we know better. From such weakness will be created the new heaven and the new earth, and the promise of eternity with God.

Living the Lord's Prayer

There is nothing in the Lord's Prayer to which a Jew or Moslem (or anyone believing in God's fatherhood) could object. It is not an exclusively Christian prayer. Its author, after all, was a Jew who taught his prayer to Jews. When, six centuries later, Mohammed drew from the traditions of Judaism and Christianity to create a faith for his own people, the Prophet sustained the sentiments expressed in Jesus' prayer.

The Christian faith, however, subordinates Jesus' prowess as a teacher to his effectiveness as an *actor*—specifically as redeemer of humankind. Jesus did not simply teach us to pray; he answered our prayer by saving us from ourselves and for his Father. Christianity believes that Jesus' *life* was his prayer, as were his death and resurrection in glory, paving our way to join him and our creator for eternity.

Accordingly, a Christian does not regard Jesus of Nazareth as a model from the past but instead insists: I know my redeemer *lives*. The Christian faith proclaims that the saving act of Jesus on the cross two millennia ago was never consigned to the dustbins of history but is effective now and operative until the end of time. For the Christian, Jesus is the permanent key to breaking God's silence.

I will be the first to admit that the Christian explanation of what Jesus accomplished in his brief life on earth is more complicated than it need be, but that is because redemption is ultimately a mystery that theologians have obscured by two thousand years of disputatious jargon. What is clear is that the incarnation (God becoming man) and the redemption (God saving humankind) are considered facts by Christians, and are the genius of Christianity, making it distinctive among the world's religions. They explain why Jesus is the best pray-er, not in his own interest, but for all of God's creatures. Christians believe that their efforts at prayer would be futile without his. He is the living substance of prayer, the Word made flesh.

Other faiths, not content with mental words alone, also give physical expression to their prayers. Jews pray aloud and from the printed page. Moslems rub their prayers into their faces to absorb them. Hindus in India paint daily prayers in the entrances to their homes. Buddhists assume prayerful physical postures.

Christians uniquely follow someone they believe was simultaneously Son of Man and Son of God—living proof that the divine and the merely human can not only coexist but be integrated. In the hands of a novelist, a creature who was at once God and man would be a schizophrenic monster, racked with unbearable inner tensions. In real life, however, Jesus placed his humanity totally before the will of his Father, proving that people really are made in God's image and are capable of acting with integrity.

In the process, however, Jesus underwent agonies of doubt and anticipation, as well as betrayal by his friends, then embraced the pain and desolation of the cross. Because he was successful, this sad story became the good news of the gospel.

Reconciling Humanity to God

Dramatic as the external events of Jesus' life are, it is *within* him that redemption is played out and humanity is reconciled to its creator. Jesus laid down his life for his friends, who include all God's creatures. Being who he was, loving and obedient to the death, he was raised up, conquering death not only for himself but for everyone who, like him, seeks God's will.

I concede that this scenario is the stuff of faith, not of total understanding, but it is central, and its significance to the man or woman of faith is crystal clear. When you pray, approaching your creator, you travel a well-marked road already paved by Jesus, who once, for all time and all people, reconciled humanity with divinity and time with eternity. Jesus' self-sacrifice was accepted and benefits everyone. When the Christian prays, he or she enters into the saving act of Jesus, who is now Christ and Lord in glory. Prayer is therefore not a do-it-yourself exercise. Jesus has already done all that needs to be done for us; what is required is only that we join our prayer to his.

The key to effective prayer as a Christian is nothing other than *intention:* binding your prayer to Jesus' life prayer, with all that entails. To pray with Jesus assumes a willingness to sacrifice oneself, and it means praying not for ourselves alone but for everyone, even our enemies.

Praying in the Church and in the Spirit

Thus far I have alluded infrequently to the communal prayer of the church, which in its liturgy reenacts the redemptive work of Jesus. But in my earlier book, *Growing in Faith,* I emphasized the need for believers to pray together rather than pretend a purely solo relationship with God. Judaism's clear preference for congregational (over private) prayer reflects that ancient faith's suspicion of self-serving petitions and illustrates its insistence that the one God is the God of all. Christianity encourages personal prayer as an adjunct to communal worship, but cautions that God is no one believer's private possession—the heresy that fosters religious fanaticism. You and I share the common fate made possible by the sacrifice of Jesus for all humankind.

The church therefore insists that no prayer can be effective unless it enters into the prayer of Christ and includes everyone—something it facilitates through common worship and the sacraments. Jesus promised that whenever two or three are gathered together in his name, he will be there as well, joining them. Whoever would be effective in prayer cannot be a loner but must to some extent be a joiner. Even the hermit joins his solitary prayer with humanity and for humanity.

In the final analysis, personal prayer is not a lonely enterprise at all: "I shall ask the Father to give you someone else to stand by you, to be with you always. I mean the Spirit . . . you recognize him, for he is with you now and will be in your hearts. I am not going to leave you alone in the world . . . " (John 14:16–18). This is Jesus' promise to his friends: that God's Spirit will dwell within us, acting as our advocate, ensuring that our prayers are effective, because they are not ours alone. We pray the prayer of Jesus, and it is God's Spirit who prays within us.

You are never alone in personal prayer. Instead, the Father listens, the Son saves, and the Spirit prays within you. The Lord's Prayer calls down grace on anyone who calls God Father—which is to say all of us. As Robert Louis Stevenson prayed confidently before his death,

> Grant that we here before thee may be set free from the fear of vicissitude and the fear of death, may finish what remains before us of our course without dishonor to ourselves or hurt to others; and, when the day comes, may die in peace. Deliver us from fear and favor: from mean hopes and cheap pleasures. Have mercy on each in his deficiency; let him not be cast down. Support the stumbling on the way, and give at last rest to the weary.

7

A Brief History of Prayer

Prayer in the pagan world was stiff, formal, and formulaic, as befitted a conversation that commenced, in effect, with "To whom it may concern." Pagan prayer flattered and cajoled, assuming that gods, like politicians, were vain and self-serving. Toadying to dieties, of course, was not flattering to them; it was manipulative. But then pagans did not really seek their gods' friendship—only their favor.

Religion is, by definition, the relationship of God and humanity. In the biblical myth, the first man and woman converse with God in the Garden of Eden. It is clearly an unequal relationship, but a caring one. The relationship cracked when our first parents tired of dependency and made an abortive stab at going it alone. God confirmed their isolation, and they found themselves in solitude without God to talk to.

A later story in Genesis is also instructive. In a misconceived attempt to reach God, an ancient people built a tower to the heavens, but before it could be completed, the builders lost the ability to communicate with one another. They found themselves speaking different languages, unable to coordinate their attempts to construct a ladder to heaven. Where once man and woman conversed easily with God, now mankind had been reduced to babbling.

Effective Prayer

Effective prayer began when God himself reopened the conversation after Eden, most notably with the patriarch Abraham and his immediate progeny. This is the conversation that has continued through the successive traditions of Judaism, Christianity, and Islam. It has not always been an easy conversation. In his revelation God was often demanding and unrelenting. Yet the restored dialogue between God and humanity is the very antithesis of formality. The patriarchs, the kings, and the prophets address God in awe, but with ease.

The Psalms, consisting of 150 prayers set to music (since lost) were attributed to King David, who lived a thousand years before the birth of Jesus. These prayerful songs demonstrate the character of the restored conversation and continue three thousand years later to be models of prayer. In their candor, the Psalms were undoubtedly more assured and sophisticated than the common prayer of the time, but David, who inspired them, was a king in God's favor and could presume to address God with confidence.

A thousand years later, Jesus speaks to the Father as to someone he knows intimately. Once Jesus returned to his Father, further revelation became unnecessary; that has led some to worry that God is no longer holding up his end of the conversation but has fallen silent. It is more correct to acknowledge that, following all that Jesus said and did, God has nothing *new* to say. But the faithful are not abandoned. Jesus left his followers the legacy of his church and the power of the Holy Spirit. "I will not leave you orphans," Christ promised when he returned to the Father. Christians believe the Father has adopted us through the Spirit of adoption. Acting within God's church and within each believer, the Spirit assures the efficacy of prayer by praying in and through each of us. This prompted the twentieth-century missionary Amy Carmichael to pray:

Holy Spirit
think through me

        till your ideas
        are my ideas.

It is a sentiment expressed poetically by Christina Rossetti:

> As the wind is thy symbol
> so forward our goings.
> As the dove
> so launch us heavenwards.
> As water
> so purify our spirits.
> As a cloud
> so abate our temptations.
> As dew
> so revive our languor.
> As fire
> so purge our dross.

Early Instructions for Prayer

The *Letter to Diognetus,* which is contained in a second-century collection of writings by the Apostolic Fathers, marveled over the earliest Christians' lack of exclusivity in society: "Christians do not form a separate group marked off from other people by land, language or custom; they do not live in towns of their own nor speak a foreign tongue nor follow a special way of life . . . In their dress and way of living and general outward behavior they conform to native usage." But, he adds, "they are pilgrims . . . They live on the earth but their city is in heaven."

This sense of temporary exile marks Christian consciousness to this day, but it was especially keen among the earliest Christians, who expected Jesus' return to be imminent. They prayed often and expectantly. However, by the time of Clement of Alexandria, who died before 216 A.D., living witnesses to Jesus had long since died. Reasoning that the faithful needed to lengthen their perspective, Clement turned his attention to "how the Christian is to overcome the world while remaining in it." He concluded that the believer must make his whole life a prayer, living in constant consciousness of God's presence.

Clement of Alexandria characterized life in the early Christian community as including fixed hours of devotion each day, "canticles of praise" and scripture readings before meals and sleep, "interior" (meditative) prayers during the night, and frequent lifting of one's eyes and hands toward heaven. The *Didache*, a manual of instructions also contained in the writings of the Apostolic Fathers, prescribed prayer three times daily. Origen, an early church father also from Alexandria, confirmed that the Lord's Prayer was the standard. By the third century, however, prescriptions for prayer became mannered and fussy. The church father Tertullian of Carthage advised: Do not sit. Raise hands only modestly. Pray aloud but not loudly. Kneel at morning prayer. Women shall cover their heads. Pray morning and night and three times in between, but also before meals and one's bath.

The anonymous author of the *Shepherd of Hermas* added that prayer should be joined to fasting. The martyr Cyprian further linked prayer to almsgiving. Hippolytus of Rome in his *Apostolic Tradition* (c. 215) encouraged Christians to meditate on the life of Jesus and on God's work of redemption throughout the day, then rise at midnight to celebrate all creation's song of praise at the approaching dawn and Jesus' second coming.

Contemporary Christians would regard midnight prayer daunting. But in the centuries before artificial lighting, the nights were longer than anyone's need for sleep, and the darkness had the advantage of offering few distractions from one's thoughts. Unlike the present, when we time our lives by the minute with a watch on our wrist, earlier peoples toiled through the daylight hours with a sense of almost unbroken time. To pause in midmorning, midday, and midafternoon (the third, sixth, and ninth hours) for contemplation of life's bigger picture and one's place in it was not so much tedious as a break from monotony.

Do We Pray to Jesus?

For a time in the early church, it was disputed whether Jesus himself was a proper object of prayer. Origen argued that prayers ought properly to begin and end "with the praise and glorification of the Father, through Jesus Christ and the Holy Spirit," *excluding* prayers addressed directly to Jesus—Origen's argument being that "if one wishes to pray aright one must not pray to him who is himself praying . . . whom the Father has appointed high priest and mediator."

While Origen had a theological point, it was too fine for Christian tradition to follow it consistently. The great early hymns still in use today—the *Gloria in Excelsis* (Glory to God in the Highest) and *Te Deum* (We Praise Thee O God)—address Jesus as well as the Father. Approaching their execution, the Christians known as the Abitena martyrs cried out directly to their crucified Lord: "O Christ, the Lord, let us not be confounded. Son of God, come to our aid; help, O Christ; have pity, Lord Christ; give us courage to suffer." In our time the spirituals stemming from the African American experience perpetuate a preference for praying directly to Jesus. Grammy Award–winning composer (and Pentecostal pastor) Walter Hawkins composed this prayer in 1976:

> Dear Jesus, I love you.
> Dear Jesus, I love you.
> You're a friend of mine.
> You supply my every need.
> My hungry soul You feed.
> I'm aware You are my source
> From which all blessings flow,
> And with this thought in mind
> I know just where to go.

Origen was persuasive, however, in arguing that prayer is effective precisely *because* of Jesus. Early Christians concluded their prayers with the phrase "through Christ our Lord" to underline Jesus' role in their redemption. Whether or not he was directly addressed, Jesus became the object of every Christian's meditations; this led Hippolytus to claim: "If you perform these things . . . you will not be tempted or come to grief, since in every event you keep Christ before your eyes."

Nonbelievers regard the cross as a negative symbol and a depressing focus for prayer, on the order of a scaffold or an electric chair. Yet the earliest Christians viewed the cross as the symbol not of Jesus' humiliation but of his victory over sin and death. They literally traced the cross on one another as greeting and blessing. By the second century, Christians commonly painted or fixed a cross on the east wall of their houses, facing the rising sun, which they welcomed as a daily reminder of their risen savior.

In the early church, ordinary believers, however devout, had real-world responsibilities that limited their time for prayer. But by the fourth century, unmarried men and women began to retreat from the cities to pursue solitary lives of prayer, following the example of Jesus' sojourn in the desert before he began his ministry. In his quest for a life of ceaseless prayer, the Syrian hermit Lucius struck upon the device of paying others to pray on his behalf while he was eating or sleeping.

The discipline of ceaseless prayer suggests that the hermits were chanting all day long, when in fact their prayer was simple but focused. The early Eastern monk Abba Macarius taught his followers to repeat simple phrases: "Have pity on me," "Help me." In prayer's simplest form, Christians repeat Jesus' name over and over again. In the seventh century John Climacus, the great teacher of Eastern Christianity, advised: "If you find consolation or a sense of contrition in a single word of your prayer, dwell upon it, for your angel guardian is at your side and is praying with you."

Prayer Without Scripture

Contrary to modern practice, the rich tradition of prayer in the earliest centuries of Christianity developed without the easy availability of the Bible. In the ancient world, the book Christians know as the Old Testament was typically available to Jews in the synagogues and to scholars. Although portions of the New Testament circulated widely, the full text was not fully compiled and sanctioned by the church until well into the fifth century. Prayer closely connected to scripture is sounder and richer than improvization, but we run the risk of concentrating on reading and analysis when, at times, we might better respond to God with a word or two. Prayerful study is important, but it is not the same thing as prayer.

This explains why so many of the prayers I have included in this book are thoughtful, spontaneous expressions that personalize the Bible's good news but are not its prisoners. My Virginia neighbor Marjorie Holmes, for example, prays from her own real-life situation:

I've got to talk to somebody, God.

I'm worried, I'm unhappy. I feel inadequate so often, hopeless, defeated, afraid.

Or again I'm so filled with delight I want to run into the streets proclaiming, "Stop, world, listen! Hear this wonderful thing."

But nobody pauses to listen, out there or here—here in the very house where I live. Even those closest to me are so busy, so absorbed in their own concerns.

They nod and murmur and make an effort to share it, but they can't; I know they can't before I begin.

There are all these walls between us—husband and wife, parent and child, neighbor and neighbor, friend and friend. Walls of self. Walls of silence, Even walls of words. For even when we try to talk to each other new walls begin to rise. We camouflage, we hold back, we make ourselves sound better than we really are. Or we are shocked and hurt by what is revealed. Or we sit privately in judgment, criticizing even when we pretend to agree. But with you, Lord, there are no walls.

You, who made me, know my deepest emotions, my most secret thoughts. You know the good of me and the bad of me, you already understand . . .

Once Christianity came out of hiding in the fourth century following the Peace of Constantine, public prayer—the liturgy—blossomed aboveground. Communal prayer in turn enriched private devotion. Now that the faith was not only tolerated by government but embraced by the emperor as his personal religion, churches multiplied and daily prayer services joined the traditional Sunday Eucharist. The agape was revived, wherein wealthy Christians invited their poorer neighbors to their homes for a meal reenacting Jesus' last supper with his apostles. Typically, a cleric was present at these holy feasts, which began with a blessing of the light and recitation of psalms, concluding with a joyful "Alleluia."

Simple morning and evening observances were the precursors of the daily recitation in cathedral churches of Matins and Vespers—a practice that persists to this day. With the rise of the monastic movement, additional hours of communal prayer would fill the day between morning and evening devotions.

Matins commenced before sunrise and ushered in the day. Early rising was not as onerous as we might imagine, because without light the night was long, and the day's work could not begin until sunrise. Surprisingly, these prayer services were more attractive to laypeople than to the clergy, who had to be assigned to them. In fourth-century Gaul, however, it was not unusual for Vespers to be held in a cathedral with no clergy present. These daily cathedral services became effective schools of prayer. Although the faithful were not expected to memorize the psalms, in fact they did by sheer rote, assisted by the practice of *responsorial* prayer, in which the congregation recited only alternate verses.

The Psalms

Here is the *morning* prayer, (Psalm 62), with asterisks indicating phrasing for communal plainchant:

My soul truly waiteth still upon God; * for of him cometh my salvation.
He verily is my strength and my salvation; * he is my defence, so that I shall not greatly fall.
How long will ye imagine mischief against every man? * Ye shall be slain all the sort of you; yea, as a tottering wall shall ye be, and like a broken hedge.
Their device is only how to put him out whom God will exalt; * their delight is in lies; they give good words with their mouth, but curse with their heart.
Nevertheless, my soul, wait thou still upon God; * for my hope is in him.
He truly is my strength and my salvation; * he is my defence, so that I shall not fall.
In God is my health and my glory; * the rock of my might; and in God is my trust.
O put your trust in him alway, ye people; * pour out your hearts before him, for God is our hope.
As for the children of men, they are but vanity; the children of men are deceitful; * upon the weights they are altogether lighter than vanity itself.
O trust not in wrong and robbery; give not yourselves unto vanity: * if riches increase, set not your heart upon them.
God spake once, and twice I have also heard the same, * that power belongeth unto God;
And that thou, Lord, art merciful; * for thou rewardest every man according to his work.

And the *evening* prayer, Psalm 140:

Deliver me, O LORD, from the evil man; * and preserve me
from the wicked man;
Who imagine mischief in their hearts, * and stir up strife all
the day long.
They have sharpened their tongues like a serpent; * adder's
poison is under their lips.
Keep me, O LORD, from the hands of the ungodly; * preserve
me from the wicked men, who are purposed to overthrow my
goings.
The proud have laid a snare for me, and spread a net abroad
with cords; * yea, and set traps in my way.
I said unto the LORD, Thou art my God, * hear the voice of my
prayers, O LORD.
O LORD God, thou strength of my health; * thou hast covered
my head in the day of battle.
Let not the ungodly have his desire, O LORD; * let not his mischievous imagination prosper, lest they be too proud.
Let the mischief of their own lips fall upon the head of them *
that compass me about.
Let hot burning coals fall upon them; * let them be cast into
the fire, and into the pit, that they never rise up again.
A man full of words shall not prosper upon the earth: * evil
shall hunt the wicked person to overthrow him.
Sure I am that the LORD will avenge the poor, * and maintain
the cause of the helpless.
The righteous also shall give thanks unto thy Name; * and the
just shall continue in thy sight.

The church father Caesarius of Arles stated that everyone
knew Psalm 103 ("Praise the Lord, O my soul"), Psalm 50 ("The
Lord, even the most mighty God, hath spoken"), and Psalm 90
("Lord, thou hast been our refuge"). In Naples in the fourth
century, candidates for baptism were required to memorize
Psalm 116 ("My delight is in the Lord, because he has heard my

prayer") and Psalm 23 ("The Lord is my shepherd"). Great litanies were composed, chains of prayers of petition, to which the
faithful responded, "Have mercy on us," and, "Hear us."

Nowhere in the New Testament could be found a treasury of
prayer so rich and ready-made for public devotion as the
Psalms. They constituted a combined prayer book and a hymnal, for they were reset to music—the unaccompanied plain
(or Gregorian) chant. The psalms' shortcomings were that
they were not Christian at all, but rather reflected the spirit of
a warrior king troubled by his political adversaries. One can
hardly imagine the psalms' inspiration, King David the giant
killer, embracing the Sermon on the Mount and loving his enemies. Nevertheless, for want of a ready alternative, the early
church "baptized" the psalms and proceeded to read them in
the context of Jesus. Where David prayed to defeat his political
enemies, Christians used the psalms he inspired to ask God's
help in conquering their own sins. Saint Augustine devoted an
entire book to reinterpreting all 150 psalms in the light of
Christ.

Personal and Public Prayer

While this development of devotion was public, there was also
clearer counsel about personal prayer. Saint Augustine wrote a
treatise in which he characterized personal devotion as yearning for the blessed life in faith, hope, and love. He accepted literally Paul's command that we "pray always" but leaned to the
Eastern tradition of brief, ejaculatory phrases as an effective
way to maintain devotion. Augustine confirmed that the Lord's
Prayer contains all that we need to pray for, and he repeated
Saint Paul's warning that we do not really know what to ask for
in prayer. Accordingly, he counseled Christians not to be too
specific in their petitions, but rather to seek God's will. Augustine insisted that God answers every prayer by giving what is
best for our spiritual welfare, but he questioned whether one

person's prayer for another automatically purchases God's favor. Augustine's *Confessions,* written in the form of an autobiography, can be read as one long self-critical and devoted prayer.

The development of a comprehensive and official order of daily prayer (the Divine Office) was left to the monasteries, where a disciplined communal life free of commercial and family responsibility afforded the time and leisure to schedule frequent formal prayer. From the church's infancy there have always been devout Christians for whom morning and evening prayer were insufficient—notably hermits and consecrated virgins. Although they prefigured stable communities of monks and nuns, in the newly aboveground church they were only unorganized individuals who frequented services. By the year 400, daily services in Jerusalem had already been augmented by prayers at midday (Sext) and midafternoon (None), as well as midmorning (Terce) in Lent. Matins and Vespers, rather than expanding themselves, spun off new hours of devotion, which would become known as Prime, Terce, and Compline.

The monastic movement developed in isolated areas outside cities, coincidental with the decline of the cities and the barbarian invasions, but monastic prayer life can be traced to the institution of basilica monasteries in those cities as early as the fourth century in Caesaria and the mid-fifth century in Rome. By the eighth century there were sixty houses of perpetual prayer in Rome alone. The clergy of these basilicas were forerunners of the canons of collegiate and cathedral chapters that exist to our day. What is noteworthy is that the church had found an official way to perpetuate prayer, by setting aside portions of seven hours, or periods from predawn to nightfall, and including brief lessons for meditation.

The development of this Divine Office, or official public prayer, incorporating lessons from scripture, helped to counteract the eccentricities and ignorance of the solitaries. Praying in common even in the cities required living at least part of the time in the company of others—a healthy test of the Christian imperative to love one another and a healthy counterbalance to the temptation of the devout to have God all to themselves. But it is instructive that the church's official prayer, while it thrived in the remote monasteries of celibates who found city life antagonistic to devotion, was actually imported from the cities, where it originated as the prayer life of married men and women, and children as well. Monastic prayer was not the invention of the monasteries or even of the clergy, but of the urban laity.

In our own time the eminent pollster George Gallup Jr. is an articulate exponent of praying in groups to ensure that personal prayer does not degenerate into selfish eccentricity:

> There's something particularly powerful about prayer in a group; there is a sort of corrective mechanism. When you're discussing things and you're praying for things, it's important to have other people's insights, and their prayer, and their contact with God. You can bounce things off people; they can say, "Well, George, really; perhaps *this* is what is happening." In a sense they're a sounding board. You could go off on the wrong tack if you're alone, but when you're with a group, it keeps you from falling into error in your perceptions of what kind of things you should be doing . . . We live in a disjointed, impersonal society, a fragmented society, and small groups provide one way for people to come back together.

Progressive Prayer

In monasteries prayer was everyone's principal occupation. Any commercial activity was pursued as a sideline to sustain life until, in death, one was called to join one's savior. With a lifetime of prayer to contemplate, the monk had to keep goals in mind. In his *Institutes* (c. 430), John Cassian, founder of Saint Victor in Marseilles, laid out a progressive plan of prayer that he had absorbed in a decade living with anchorites in the

Egyptian desert. Affirming that prayer is the defining task of the monk, Cassian argued that its success rests on controlling one's appetites and passions while renouncing worldly interests—not necessarily as evils but as distractions from the task at hand. Noting that there are as many kinds of prayer as there are persons praying, Cassian established progressive goals. First, the monk must seek God's *forgiveness*, then *renunciation* of the world, followed by prayer for *others*, ending in the noblest prayer—that of *thanksgiving*. In order to engender a habit of continuous prayer, Cassian urged monks to model themselves on the anchorites, who repeated, over and over again, the simple request "God, come to my aid; Lord, hasten to help me." According to Cassian, this persistent reaffirmation of one's dependence on God leads to poverty of spirit. With perfect compunction, prayer can reach a level of communication with God that dispenses altogether with words or images but, as with lovers, contents itself with looks and sighs. Cassian affirmed that the goal of prayer is nothing except love.

Mainstream monasticism in Europe developed from the practical *Rule* of Saint Benedict (died c. 543), who aimed at establishing economically self-sustaining single-sex communities of unmarried men and women possessing sufficient discipline to ensure a peaceful common life. Solitary devotion was to occupy even those hours not dedicated to physical labor or to communal prayer in choir. In the long daylit hours of summer, for example, Saint Benedict called for three hours of labor followed by two hours of reading and meditation before the midday meal. Benedict's prescription of scripture reading to improve one's prayer was in marked contrast to the often eccentric practices of the desert anchorites. As we now know, it was the monasteries that protected the riches of ancient learning through the Dark Ages, not as museums, but as centers of active scholarship. Prayer in the monasteries was not at all simpleminded; it was thoughtful, contemplative, and closely linked to God's revelation.

A New Pessimism

Monasticism in Ireland added three elements to common prayer: the creation of long litanies seeking divine protection, the practice of reading all (or practically all) of the psalms each day, and the penitential practice of praying with arms outstretched. While vigorous and vital, Irish monastic devotion contained something of an ordeal. Personal prayer came to stress length over quality, favoring sin consciousness as the driving motive of devotion. Like Judaism, Irish monasticism accorded greater value to personal prayer pronounced aloud than in one's heart.

Orthodoxy was victorious in defending Jesus' divinity, but at the grave expense of placing a distance between humankind and its divine savior. According to the German liturgist Josef Jungmann, "When faith was no longer actively conscious of the redemption and of the mediation effected by Christ, when the vast distance separating man from God oppressed his spirit with little now to mitigate the burden, the consciousness of his misery and sinfulness must have been overwhelming."

At the Synod of Tours (A.D. 813), Christians were directed for the first time to pray on their knees and to "crave God's mercy and the forgiveness of sins." By the ninth century the Christian empire of Charlemagne had restored much of the civility of Roman civilization but retained only a fragile sense of redemption by Jesus. Joy had been replaced by guilt. Along with a pervasive preoccupation with sin came the tendency to bypass Jesus and seek more accessible mediators with God, among them angels, martyrs, and—most notably—Mary, the mother of Jesus. Relics of the saints took on a new importance. The English theologian Alcuin taught the emperor Charlemagne a rigorous devotion, specifying prayer focused on the sufferings of Jesus to aggravate a sense of sin rather than the joy of resurrection and redemption. Prayer became hesitant and uncertain. Here is the anxious conclusion to a prayer in the ninth-century *Sacramentary* of Amiens: "This is the faith by which I am expressing belief in you. If I am believing properly, all is well. But in case something is lacking, I pray you not to regard the words I have spoken but what I wished to say."

Dividing the Trinity

In a further development, orthodoxy's successful defense of the Trinity led popular piety in the early Middle Ages to address similar prayers to *each* divine person, hedging one's bets by praying to Father, Son, and Holy Spirit in turn. This ostensibly afforded the devout Christian three chances rather than one at contacting God, just in case one of the persons was not listening. Christians clearly had lost not only their confidence but also their awareness of the Trinitarian dimension of prayer: *to* the Father *through* Christ *in* the Spirit.

Prayer was further diluted by the growing demand in the monasteries to pray for the abbey's benefactors rather than for oneself and for the needy. The motive was mercenary. In early monasticism the monks had constructed the buildings with their own hands, but by the ninth century monastic buildings were the gift legacies of wealthy landowners. The payback for their generosity increasingly took the form of prayer specifically to aid their benefactors, alive or dead. Quantity increasingly replaced quality, and by the eleventh century monks were expected to chant between 138 and 215 psalms every day. Since there are only 150 psalms, it meant a demand in some places to repeat prayers the same day. By contrast, the founder of Western monasticism, Saint Benedict, had spread this burden over the entire week.

As monastic prayer lengthened it also diverged from the devotion of ordinary Christians. Not possessing copies of the psalms, the average Christian had to be content with repeated rote renderings of the Lord's Prayer and the Apostles' Creed, together with prostrations and the repetition of brief phrases asking God's mercy and forgiveness. Wealthy lay men and women had access to prayer books that offered the dubious distinction of separate prayers addressed to each of the divine persons, plus prayers invoking the mediation of more than two hundred saints, each by name.

The New Mood

Unaccountably, the spiritual mood of Christians changed again at the turn of the eleventh into the twelfth century. I have already noted the shift of attention away from Christ's work of redemption, the victory of the cross, and the risen Lord presiding over a new kingdom and new creation. Now the focus of Christian devotion shifted again—away from Easter's glory to the innocence of Christmas and the tragedy of Good Friday, and to purely human details of Jesus's life. At first blush this development appears to be a welcome humanizing of faith. We think of Francis of Assisi celebrating the babe of Bethlehem and the flowering of nature as God's creation. On balance, however, Christian piety developed an unhealthy fixation on the life and death of Jesus with scant regard to its victorious final chapter. Popular devotion proceeded as if the conclusion of the story of Jesus were the crucifixion. Prayer fixed increasingly on the cross itself—an ofttimes morbid fascination that led to Christians blaming themselves personally for Jesus' torture and execution.

Consider, for example, Saint Anselm's determination to imbue a penitential attitude in the devout Christian by dramatizing the agonies of the redeemer. He demanded of his fellow Christians: "How is it possible that the sword of grief did not pierce you also? Were you not present [at the crucifixion] too and suffered the lance to pierce the Redeemer's heart? . . . How came it that you were not drunk with bitter tears as he drank the bitter gall?"

The Crusades were but one outcome of this new fixation on the cross. Christians were exhorted by the reformist Peter

Damian (d. 1072) to devotion to Jesus' five wounds: "The body of the Lord is pierced five times over that we may be healed from the sins that enter through our five senses." It did not take long for Christians to discover the drawbacks to praying to Jesus as if he were eternally affixed to his cross in agony. But rather than revive the joy of redemption celebrated by the primitive church, they sought ways of coping with their guilt. Typically, this took the form of seeking the intercession of the mother of Jesus and the saints.

The rosary was the product of the eleventh and twelfth centuries, its beads assisting with repetitive prayer intended ideally as background to meditation on aspects of the Virgin's and the savior's lives. As the Divine Office was more and more restricted to the monasteries, the rosary became the people's substitute psalter. Portable and inexpensive, it was ideal for the illiterate or for anyone without access to a book—which is to say, for the majority of Christians.

The rosary was first mentioned in A.D. 1140 as a counting device that facilitated repetitions of the Lord's Prayer in place of the 150 psalms. It developed into a string of fifty beads, each signaling the recitation of a Hail Mary, interrupted after every tenth prayer by the Lord's Prayer. So constituted, the rosary became a fixture of Catholic devotion until after the Second Vatican Council in the early 1960s. For our understanding of the development of prayer, what is revealing is that the rosary prescribed ten prayers to Jesus' mortal mother for every prayer addressed to his divine Father.

Saints and Relics

Devotion to the saints was abetted by countless relics given prominence in the churches and the collections of wealthy Christians. There had always been traffic in wood chips claimed to be from the cross on which Jesus died. Even today there is a fascination among believers and nonbelievers alike that the shroud of Turin may have enclosed the dead Jesus and might bear his imprint. As the Middle Ages progressed, the relics of the saints abounded. Affluent Christians collected them as a hobbyist today might seek rare coins or stamps. Typically, relics consisted of a portion of a saint's body (hair, bone, or nail), clothing, or something the blessed one used in life. As a young theological student in Paris, I prayed in a twelfth-century Latin Quarter church whose side altar held the entire body of an obscure thousand-year-old saint encased in glass.

Despite these developments, two healthy notes were struck as Christian devotion entered its second millennium. One was a weakening of the compulsive need to address each of the three divine persons. The other was a revival of the sacrament of Penance as a lifelong refuge offering God's forgiveness and a practical antidote to morbid guilt.

Bernard of Clairvaux (d. 1153) and Francis of Assisi (d. 1226) both embraced the new piety that focused on Jesus' life and death rather than his resurrection and kingdom. But they avoided the morbidity of others by drawing attention to Jesus' sacred humanity during his life and by defining the Christian vocation as the imitation of Christ in his virtue, love, and sufferings. It was Francis who popularized the feast of Christmas in A.D. 1223 to welcome anew the babe of Bethlehem, reborn to every age. At the end of his life, however, Francis reflected the spirit of his era by assuming the five death wounds of the suffering savior on his own body.

Until the appearance of Francis and his fellow friar Saint Dominic, prayer life had developed sophistication in the monasteries at the expense of ignorance and superstition in the everyday world of most believers. The two friars, each the founder of vast new religious families not confined to monasteries, accelerated the growth of "third orders"—loose confraternities of devout lay Christians determined to lead lives of prayer in the everyday world. For those who could read Latin, books of hours were published between the thirteenth and sixteenth centuries. These were richly illustrated prayer books that leaned heavily on the psalms but also contained other prayers and meditations. After the invention of moveable type, these prayer books became legion.

Popular Devotion

For unlettered Christians in the Middle Ages, devotional life centered on mental repetition of familiar prayers and recitation in common of The Lord's Prayer and the Creed. There was vocal prayer at Mass on Sundays and on holy days, which multiplied to one almost every week of the year. Even the most devout Christians in the Age of Faith were accustomed to receive the sacred bread and wine no more often than three times a year—a rationing of the Eucharist that prompted the visual adoration of Christ in the host, displayed on the altar but unconsumed. The reservation of the consecrated bread was originally intended to provide *viaticum* for the sick and dying. But in time it served to underline Christ's "real presence" in Catholic, high Anglican, and Orthodox churches—a practice that persists. As a child I was taught that Jesus, confined to the host and locked in a gold container on the altar, was the "prisoner of the tabernacle."

The quality of monastic prayer declined in the centuries preceding the Reformation. At Montserrat, Abbot Cisneros (d. 1510) instructed his monks to actively meditate on the life of Christ while reciting the psalms in common—a practice that ensured inattention to the meaning of the psalms themselves and invited daydreaming. In 1534 Cardinal Quiñonez issued a new breviary filled with welcome scriptural readings, but at the expense of abbreviating the psalms. The book was immensely popular, not least because it compensated for widespread ignorance of the Bible. But it served to underline the decline of the psalms to little more than a kind of medieval Musak—background music for other activity. Clearly some new approach to the ongoing conversation with God was needed.

"Modern Devotion"

One approach began in what is now the Netherlands and can be traced as far back as Gerhard Groote (d. 1384), founder of the Brothers of the Common Life. The institutional church at the time was in shambles, pulled asunder by contending popes and princes. Ordinary Christians, and clerics as well, were left to their own devotional devices. The Brothers of the Common Life and their associates, the Canons of Windesheim, searched for an unencumbered path to God. By common accord they structured their worship around a simplified and unadorned daily celebration of the Eucharist, while each brother and canon developed a capacity for interior prayer. In the process they created a new piety that came to be known as the *devotio moderna,* intended not only to uplift souls but to reform a complacent church. In contrast to the chanted monastic hours, the new devotion was private and meditative, with successive days of the week specified for topics, among them God's blessings, the life of Mary, the last judgment, the saints and angels, and the life and sufferings of Jesus. To this day *The Imitation of Christ* of Thomas à Kempis remains a spiritual best-seller illustrating this method of prayer.

So too are the *Spiritual Exercises* of Ignatius of Loyola, founder of the Jesuits, first published in 1535. For Ignatius mental prayer was basic—not just an adjunct to common prayer. Indeed, the Jesuits largely dispensed with communal prayer as incompatible with their active missionary responsibilities. For centuries afterward Catholic authorities would argue that the Jesuit approach was selfish and a challenge to the pure motivation behind choral prayer—to honor God without expectation of any personal benefit. As it developed, there was no contest; meditative prayer came to complement choral prayer within monastic life. And the Jesuits themselves took pains to censure those members who aspired to the personal consolation of mystical union with God through prayer.

Effects of the Reformation

The Reformation had the salutary effect of purging nonbiblical and nonessential elements from prayer, returning devotion to simple Bible-based piety. In the wake of the Reformation, Christian humanism—both Catholic and Protestant—created new, life-affirming prayers and hymns for public worship. In the Catholic tradition, Francis de Sales (d. 1622) in his *Introduction to the Devout Life* promoted an integrated way of life based on this new optimism—a throwback to the earliest Christians' experience of redemption and new creation.

In post-Reformation Catholicism, prayer life centered on the celebration of the Eucharist and on a proliferation of services and litanies addressed to the saints and to the mother of Jesus—and to Mary's mother, Saint Ann. There were unintended distortions motivated by a perceived need to draw distinctions between Catholic and Protestant worship, resulting notably in the worship of the displayed host, long vigils in the real presence, and downplaying of the biblical basis of prayer.

Some Catholics, in an attempt to counter the displacement of prayer from Jesus to Mary, inaugurated a new devotion, to the Sacred Heart of Jesus, which began in the sixteenth century and persists to this day. The aim was to make Jesus more accessible by combining attention to his sufferings with a clear expression of his love for sinners—dramatized by the representation of the risen Christ with his pierced heart exposed. The Sacred Heart is all-forgiving and asks only for a return of love from the sinner. While this development was Christ centered, it was nevertheless a far cry from the conviction of Jesus' immediate disciples that he had won final victory over death for all, total redemption, the gift of the Holy Spirit, and the inauguration of God's kingdom.

Post-Reformation Catholic prayer books tended to take the form of vernacular aids to following the Latin Mass. In England the official *Book of Common Prayer* provided not only a guide to the Eucharistic service but also portions of the canonical hours and a complete psalter. In the American Episcopal Church, which utilizes the *Book of Common Prayer,* Sunday services alternate between the celebration of Communion and Morning Prayer—the old monastic canonical prayer adapted for use in parish churches by laypeople.

Modern prayer in the Protestant tradition is vastly more diversified and deserves its own treatment. Consider the contrast between frenzied Holy Rollers and swirling Shakers, on the one hand, and the silent and passive Quakers, on the other, each seeking by different means what Saint Paul identified as the essence of prayer—the Spirit of God praying in and through us. In the eighth chapter of his letter to the Romans, he sets the scene for prayer:

> The whole creation is on tiptoe to see the wonderful sight of the sons of God coming into their own . . . And the hope is that in the end the whole of created life will be rescued from the tyranny of change and decay, and have its share in that magnificent liberty which can only belong to the children of God! It is plain to anyone with eyes to see that at the present time all created life groans in a sort of universal travail. And it is plain, too, that we who have a foretaste of the Spirit are in a state of painful tension, while we wait for that redemption of our bodies which will mean that at last we have realised our full sonship in him . . . The Spirit of God not only maintains this hope within us, but helps us in our present limitations. For example, we do not know how to pray worthily as sons of God, but his Spirit within us is actually praying for us in those agonizing longings which never find words . . . In face of all this, what is there left to say? If God is for us, who can be against us? . . . Who would dare to accuse us, whom God has chosen? The judge himself has declared us free from sin. Who is in a position to condemn? Only Christ, and Christ died for us, Christ rose for us, Christ reigns in power for us, Christ prays for us! Can anything

separate us from the love of Christ? . . . I have become absolutely convinced that neither death nor life, neither messenger of Heaven nor monarch of earth, neither what happens today nor what may happen tomorrow, neither a power from on high nor a power from below, nor anything else in God's whole world has any power to separate us from the love of God in Jesus Christ our Lord!

Paul's is not only the earliest commentary on effective prayer: two thousand years later it may be the last word, exemplified in the text of Charles Albert Findley's gospel hymn "Stand By Me:"

> When the storms of life are raging,
> Stand by me;
> When the storms of life are raging,
> Stand by me.
> When the world is tossing me,
> like a ship upon the sea;
> Thou who rulest wind and water.
> Stand by me.
>
> In the midst of tribulation,
> Stand by me;
> In the midst of tribulation,
> Stand by me.
> When the hosts of hell assail,
> And my strength begins to fail,
> Thou who never lost a battle,
> Stand by me.
>
> In the midst of faults and failures,
> Stand by me;
> In the midst of faults and failures,
> Stand by me.
> When I do the best I can,

And my friends misunderstand,
Thou who knowest all about me,
Stand by me.
In the midst of persecution,
Stand by me;
In the midst of persecution,
Stand by me.
When my foes in battle array
Undertake to stop my way,
Thou who saved Paul and Silas,
Stand by me.

When I'm growing old and feeble,
Stand by me;
When I'm growing old and feeble,
Stand by me.
When my life becomes a burden,
And I'm nearing chilly Jordan,
O Thou "Lily of the Valley,"
Stand by me.

8

Prayer for Skeptics

"You can't pray a lie."

Mark Twain, *Huckleberry Finn*

Like many other writer, I confess to checking out the competition from time to time, and I discovered many compilations of prayers but practically no contemporary guidance on how to pray. There appears to be renewed interest in religious titles, yet the subjects of these books are largely off center, favoring channeling, out-of-body experience, and angels, among other esoterica.

The New Age movement bids fair to legitimize the occult to an extent unique in my lifetime, blurring the lines between religion and magic. As a journalist I relish needling serious editor friends (they are *all* serious!) about the practice of carrying horoscopes in their newspapers. Fortunately, the editors I admire are at least modestly uncomfortable about mixing clairvoyance with all the news that's fit to print. (If they became true believers I would worry for American journalism.)

Although this book focuses on prayer as the path to ultimate fulfillment in union with God, I suspect that many readers may not be satisfied unless their efforts at prayer clearly improve their lot and the lives of loved ones this side of eternity. With Thomas Hardy (in his poem "Mute Opinion"), they may take a show-me attitude toward prayer:

I traversed a dominion
Whose spokesmen spake out strong
Their purpose and opinion
Through pulpit, press and song.
I scarce had means to note there
A large-eyed few, and dumb,
Who thought not as those thought there
That stirred the heat and hum.

So let us grapple with legitimate problems with prayer, confronting with candor two things that all of us, believers and skeptics alike, are concerned about—the relief of suffering in the here and now and eternal life after death.

Prayer and Healing

When John the Baptist sent emissaries to his cousin to ask if he might be the long-awaited messiah, Jesus responded by asking John to judge for himself: "The blind see, and the lame walk, the lepers are cleansed, and the deaf hear, the dead rise up, and the gospel is preached to the poor."

The great nineteenth-century theologian Adolf Harnack suggested that we should be suitably astounded by Jesus' affirmation as well as sensitive to what Jesus is *not* saying:

> By the removal of misery, of need, of sickness, by these actual effects John is to see that the new time has arrived . . . Thus to the wretched, sick and poor did he address himself, but not as a moralist, and without a trace of sentimentalism . . . He never spends time in asking whether the sick one "deserves" to be cured . . . he nowhere says that sickness is a beneficent infliction, and that health has a healthy use. No, he calls sickness sickness and health health . . . He knows that advance is possible only when . . . sickness is made well.

—Quoted in William James, *Varieties of Religious Experience*

•   •   •

Considering the things that you and I pray for in the course
of our lives and those of our loved ones, health is a high priority. No wonder Jesus got people's attention. No moralizing, no
snake oil medicine for sale, no wheedling demands for payment
or even gratitude—just action! But then we must ask: after such
a dramatic start in his public life, would Jesus keep healing and
making things right to demonstrate that the kingdom had indeed arrived? And the answer is not entirely satisfactory. Jesus
indeed continued to cure, sometimes selectively, at other times
apparently randomly. But not everyone in need is made well.
He raises Lazarus from the dead, but only after weeping for the
loss of his friend. Then he goes to his own death mocked by
those who taunt: "He saved others; can't he save himself?"

Christians ever since have relied, to some extent, on God to
cure them of their afflictions. But the Jesus who rejected the
cynical invitation "Physician: cure yourself!" is obviously no
guarantor of life-giving cures for everyone in every circum-
stance. Mainstream Christianity maintains that prayer is no
magic formula and that God is not a magician. Death comes to
all; and sickness and loss, for whatever reason, while suffered privately, are shared democratically. In her poem, "A Piteous Prayer
to a Hidden God" Harriet Jacobs recalled the poignant cry of an
American slave mother at the outbreak of the Civil War:

> My Lord and Master, help me! My load is more than I can
> bear. God has hid from me, and I am left in darkness and
> misery. (Striking her breast:) I can't tell you what is in
> here! They've got all my children. Last week they took the
> last one. God only knows where they've sold her. They let
> me have her sixteen years, and then—O! O! Pray for her
> brothers and sisters! I've got nothing to live for now. God
> make my time short!

The contemporary French priest Michel Quoist expresses a
universal experience:

> Lord, do you hear me?
> I've suffered dreadfully,
> Locked in myself,
> Prisoner of myself.
> I hear nothing but my own voice,
> I see nothing but myself,
> And behind me there is nothing but suffering.
> Lord, do you hear me?

As one might expect, there are Christians who take Jesus' healing powers literally and rely on them in our own times, sometimes exclusively. Christian Scientists, for example, take the view that illness is a lie and that everyone who mentions sickness is a liar: "God is well, and so are you!" is their claim. For these faithful, illness is a fantasy; faith effects a cure (or, more precisely, obliterates the lie along with its pain and degeneration).

Since everyone eventually dies (including Christian Scientists and Jesus himself) there is a clear limitation on what one can expect from prayer for recovery, yet this is the frequent and intense demand of our petitions. Is it bogus?

An Affirmation of Prayer

Nearly a century ago, the American philosopher-psychologist William James affirmed that "if any medical fact can be considered to stand firm, it is that in certain environments prayers may contribute to recovery, and should be encouraged as a therapeutic measure." In short, prayer "works," but not predictably. James, a lifelong agnostic, nevertheless affirmed on the basis of evidence that prayer is pragmatic. But what use is that to those of us who put our total trust in a personal God?

Scripture is clear that the apostles were able to cure the sick: "They shall lay hands on the sick and they shall recover (Mark 16:18). But following Jesus' example, the apostles were not systematic about doctoring, instead employing their power of healing to draw attention to the kingdom. For whatever reason, this dramatic ability did not pass automatically to future Christian generations. Still, Christianity through the centuries has consistently called for healing though prayer and in the sacrament of the Anointing of the Sick, which, far from being last rites, calls on God's power to restore life and health. Along with praying for cures, the church devoted itself to providing care for the ill through hospices and medicine. Even today the church in the United States competes with government by sponsoring the largest system of private hospitals anywhere.

William James was persuaded by the evidence that faith works cures, but he assigned no apparent supernatural cause to the healing, preferring an explanation of *self*-healing through positive attitudes supported by religious faith. Unfortunately, we have now endured an entire century in which "positive thinking" has been prescribed as the remedy for every sort of ill from cancer to acne and in which faith healing has come to be connected in the popular mind with the sleaziest sort of tent revivalism. It is time to clear the air.

Catholics, traditionally suspected of superstition and credulity, are, in fact, highly skeptical of the claims of faith healers. But some Catholic priests appear to have extraordinary success in praying for the sick. Father Ralph DiOrio, a priest in Worcester, Massachusetts, began in 1976 to witness dramatic cures in those he touched and prayed for. Despite his success, in his book *A Call to Heal* (Doubleday, 1982) he warns not only against substituting prayer for physicians, but also against assuming that the faith or goodness of the person healed is the cause of the cure. Positive thinking, he grants, can make the difference between living and dying, but it is God who heals as he chooses. "Why are we not all healed?" he asks rhetorically. His answer: "I do not know. There is no easy answer to the problem of suffering. It will always remain a mystery, centered in the Cross. Once I laid hands on a woman who had cancer and she received an immediate healing. A year later she became sick with another ailment, namely a fever and an infection. Again I prayed with her, but the infection took its full course and she received apparently only the blessing of the Spirit."

Father DiOrio is inclined to believe that prayers for healing often fail because people do not believe God wants them to be well and are too easily resigned to illness—which returns us to the power of positive thinking!

Remember that Jesus is clear about illness—it is real and it is evil. Pain is not a punishment for one's own sins but the fallout from original sin—wholly democratic and repugnant. With the obvious exception of Jesus' own redemptive death, human suffering is not necessarily redemptive. It may on occasion chasten the proud and convert the perverse. It may make heroes of cowards, but it is not to be wished on anyone to accomplish those goals. Suffering seldom builds character; with rare exceptions it only magnifies meanness and self-pity. When the blind and the crippled approached Jesus, they asked for more than faith and a blessing; they asked for cures. And Jesus, the supreme realist, did not chide them for being selfish or prescribe a stiff upper lip; he healed them.

Prayer and Self-Healing

Although Christians believe that suffering is the outcome of humankind's original loss of integrity, believers and skeptics alike acknowledge that (1) some people are more prone to illness than others, and that (2) some people can reduce their suffering by changing their attitudes and circumstances. Until quite recently, the practice of medicine was more art than science, and physicians noted that much illness is self-inflicted or sustained. As Carl Jung suggested: "It all depends on how we look at things and not on how they are in themselves."

What this *may* mean is that prayer can help us to heal ourselves or facilitate a doctor or a loved one helping us. Although the resultant cure may be less than technically miraculous, it is ultimately God's doing. When I am ill I become perverse. The last person I want to see is my doctor, and I snap at those who wish to help me, "Leave me alone." (Translation: leave me to stew in my own juices and wallow in self-pity.) When I most need to pray, I am disinclined, because I may improve only marginally and be that much less justified in feeling sorry for myself.

In a series of popular books, Dr. Bernie Siegel has documented the capacity of people for self-healing through love and integrity, and sometimes by prayer. The editor Norman Cousins, in an extraordinary battle against painful, presumably terminal illness, checked himself into a hotel and watched continuous Marx Brothers movies—literally laughing himself well. He went on to teach medical students at Stanford about it. Whatever restores a semblance of the integrity lost through original sin is truly the answer to all our prayers, even if the cure improbably stars Groucho, Chico, and Harpo!

Currently, the nation's top political priority is the reform of its health-care system—an enterprise that claims one-seventh of the wealth of the United States but extends unevenly to its citizens. At its best, any systemic reform will ensure that everyone has access to professional care and that families will be spared financial impoverishment from catastrophic illness. But care, however sophisticated, is not cure. We will still pray for a relief of suffering and to be made whole again.

The increasing popularity of alternative medicine at a time of extraordinary advances in mainstream medicine can be attributed less to credulity than to a growing popular sophistication about health. We all know that we will die, and we are wary of medical advances that prolong life at the expense of pain, decrepitude, and years of decline in commercial nursing homes. On reaching that point in his life, the great psychologist Bruno Bettelheim (although he had survived Dachau and Buchenwald) put a plastic bag over his head and took charge of the inevitable—something the Hemlock Society and Dr. Jack Kevorkian would like to help all of us with.

We know that bad habits, bad attitudes, bad diet, and bad living conditions make us ill—which is another way of saying that we make ourselves sick and keep ourselves from recovering. Accordingly, many of the disciplines I discussed earlier in the book that assist us to become prayerful are also embraced by people who want to get well and maintain health. In a light vein, contemporary writer Margaret Anne Huffman gives thanks for a dieter's healthy but unappetizing meal:

> Are there graces for lettuce, Lord? And low-fat, no-fat, meat-free, fun-free meals? I need you to send me words for blessing this paltry meal before me, Lord, for it is difficult to feel grateful for these skimpy portions when all I think of are the food *not* on my plate. Help me change that thought, to make peace with choosing not to eat them, for I need help in becoming the healthier person I want to be. Hold up for me a mirror of the new creation you see me to be, for I need a companion at this table, Lord.

Seeking Integrity

When we pray for health we are not asking for miracles. With all humanity we are asking for integrity—the absence of which prompted Jesus to take all the pain and confusion on himself. We are redeemed but do not realize it and seldom act on it. Instead we continue perversely to cause suffering to others and to ourselves. The Christian antidote is to take the long view but pray in the short run. When we do decide to pray for relief from suffering, we are not expressing a Buddhist longing for release from this mortal coil or an abhorrence of the flesh. The Christian view is that we are *eternally* creatures of body and spirit, sense and soul, and we will rise not as disembodied spirits but as integrated persons, body and soul in balance and at peace. For this reason we should not be too quick to distinguish healing that is physical from that which is religious. The object is the same: to reclaim the wholeness that is our primordial nature and that is the natural state of those fit to spend eternity with God. Whichever label we place on it, nothing good happens to which God is a stranger.

It is significant that five native-born American religious traditions (Mormons, Adventists, Christian Scientists, Jehovah's Witnesses, and Pentecostals) all express strong interest in religious healing. As Robert C. Fuller notes in *Alternative Medicine and American Religious Life* (Oxford, 1989),

> The metaphysical healing vision spawned by Mesmerism and Swedenborgianism continues even to this day to provide the underlying metaphors and imagery for many alternative healing philosophies. Holistic healing groups, psychic healers, New Age trance channelers, Therapeutic Touch practitioners, and even Alcoholics Anonymous have drawn heavily on this legacy of belief in the mind's capacity to draw upon higher healing energies.

At the outset of the twentieth century, William James noted in *The Will to Believe* that science had already succeeded in marginalizing religion, reducing our faith in a healing higher power to credibility only when its claims confront us as "forced, living and momentous." Illness, Fuller writes, is the one condition sufficiently "forced and momentous" to move believer and skeptic alike to seek the aid of a higher power. Noting that "modern individuals have difficulty maintaining a vital sense of self-love and suffer from emotional impoverishment," he argues that "questions concerning the . . . accessibility of God are far more fundamental to emergence of genuine spirituality than are those of instinctual renunciation and moral obedience."

Which brings us back to William James and his argument for the primacy of prayer. As he insisted in *The Varieties of Religious Experience,*

Religion is nothing if it be not the vital act by which the entire mind seeks to save itself by clinging to the principle from which it draws its life. This act is prayer, by which term I understand no vain exercise of words, no mere repetition of certain sacred formulae, but the very movement itself of the soul, putting itself in a personal relation of contact with the mysterious power of which it feels the presence—it may be even before it has a name by which to call it. Wherever this interior prayer is lacking, there is no religion; wherever, on the other hand, this prayer rises and stirs the soul, even in the absence of forms or of doctrines, we have living religion.

Praying Together

What is clear about healing prayer is that it is seldom solitary. In this book I have urged you to undertake personal prayer, but not at the expense of skimping on communal worship. We belong not only to God but to one another. At this very moment millions of Christians around the world are praying for one another and for you and me. Healing prayer is facilitated by people praying with and for one another, acknowledging Jesus' promise that "whenever two or three are gathered together in my name, there I am in the midst of them."

Without knowing them personally, I am impressed by the work of two Jesuit priest psychotherapists, Dennis and Matthew Linn, whose training for physicians is accredited by the American Medical Association. The Linns have authored a series of practical books, audio- and videotapes, anchored by a workbook, *Praying with Another for Healing* (Paulist Press, 1984). They note that the healing process appears to require the same confidence and surrender to Christ involved in personal prayer, but with the added difficulty of *mutual* abandonment to God. For best results both the person praying and the person prayed for must be of a single mind and faith. I confess to being uncomfortable with touchy-feely religion, suspecting it of sentimentality; but in extreme cases the locking of minds and spirits may be the test of self-surrender that allows God to heal the flesh.

The Light at the End of the Tunnel

Embraced by the Light is an account of an out-of-body experience during which an American woman, presumed dead after an operation, returned to life and health, but not before meeting Jesus and tasting the afterlife. The book became a best-seller, and it is tempting for skeptics and believers alike to bracket such accounts with those of people who claim to have been captured by aliens in flying saucers. Whatever credibility we lend such adventures, they confirm intense and widespread interest in an afterlife. Prayer aims at nothing less than securing this eternal intimacy with God.

If accounts of near-death and out-of-body experiences are naive and contradictory, that is no indictment of eternity. Jesus himself spoke of heaven as consisting of "many mansions," so any account of such an experience is bound to reflect the intellect, culture, and interests of the creature. When Saint Paul relates that he was "caught up to the third heaven" (2 Corinthians 12:2), he implies that the heavenly landscape offers some options.

The nation's space program chose astronauts from different backgrounds precisely because each would bring something different to the experience—ability, of course, but also receptivity. Each could be expected to report uniquely about the adventure. The idea of putting a teacher in space ended tragically, but its intent was much more than public relations for the space agency. It was assumed that she would "see" space differently and bring back a richer experience to convey to her students than, say, a military pilot or engineer might. So, too, a taste of eternity is likely to yield a different flavor for different people. Revelation is in part a product of what we bring to it.

Until I dipped into the surprisingly extensive literature, I assumed the out-of-body experience was rare. Not so. In 1982 the pollster George Gallup Jr. estimated that 23 million Americans alone had already experienced "verge of death" experiences and that 8 million reported some kind of "mystical encounter" in which they were "catapulted into another dimension." In his book *Adventures in Immortality* (McGraw-Hill, 1982), Gallup reports that the typical experience was one of "detachment, mental clarity and perspective, sense of peace and painlessness." Without putting too fine a point on it, these persons believe they visited heaven. Only 1 percent had a bad trip and believe they viewed hell. The famed "light at the end of the tunnel," incidentally, was reported by only 3 percent.

I am not suggesting that you or I pray for a near-death experience, of course. We will all die, and probably before we wish, so we pray for—not against—life. But since *eternal* life with God is what we ultimately pray for, it is worth examining these accounts for clues. Gallup reports that nearly one-third of all Americans have had what they call a religious or mystical experience, 15 million of them a feeling of union with a divine being. The out-of-body experience, then, is relatively rare compared with the experience of the impressive minority of our fellow citizens who have felt transported and touched by divinity. Many of these adventures are apparently linked to traumatic experiences, among them childbirth, accidents, and criminal attack. Whatever the occasion, vast numbers of our fellow citizens are jarred from everyday experience to taste something that smacks of eternity.

A Confession

Rest assured that I am not one among these favored millions, so I have nothing more to relate to you than God has revealed in the scriptures and you can learn from your own prayer life.

My own prayer resembles that of the contemporary French layman François Chagneau:

> You slip between my fingers
> Like the grains of sunlit sand.
> You fade away and dissolve
> Like snow in the gathering darkness.
> When the sun begins to set
> And all things fade into the peace of night,
> Perhaps then we find your kingdom
> As darkness cries out for your light.

At the same time, I am not at all certain that I feel denied by having to wait for eternity, since that affords me more time to get ready. As a young graduate student in Paris, I was too preoccupied by work and study to visit the Eiffel Tower or Versailles and would not have appreciated them had I gone. Now in late middle age, I join my wife in exploring castles and cathedrals for just a few days a year and I am immediately receptive to the echos of kings and saints.

If you are like me, your faith coexists with a skeptical outlook and you do not need visions to believe. According to Gallup, two-thirds of Americans believe in an afterlife. Only one in four denies the prospect; a small fraction are uncertain or uninterested. More than half of all Americans believe in hell and even more (70 percent) believe in the devil. As you might believe, scientists are notorious unbelievers; only 16 percent believe in an afterlife, and only half that number believe in heaven. I suspect that if my fellow journalists were polled (they hate being interviewed), they would at least match this level of skepticism—but then they are paid to be skeptical and to wear incredulity as a badge of honor (trust me: it makes for better reporting in your daily newspaper).

One might suspect that a brush with death would make us even more fearful of dying. Incredibly, two-thirds of Americans who have undergone traumatic, near-death experiences report that they either fear death less or at least fear it no more keenly. Of course death, narrowly defined, does not "hurt." What we fear most is the suffering, incapacity, and degeneration that so often precede the end. That is why I examined the matter of praying for the restoration of health before addressing prospects for the afterlife.

In Gallup's survey, the near-death experience strengthened the religious faith of 39 percent and made believers of others. Having tasted death, the survivors professed to be more philosophical and upbeat about life. Many now feel that God has a "plan" for them, which reassures them when unpredictable incidents bring pain and temporary tragedy. Some go even further and conclude that they now believe everything that happens in life has a benign purpose. This is intended to be reassuring, but if true it would follow that evil is some kind of covert good and part of God's providence.

If this were the case, Jesus would not have cured lepers but would merely have asked them to see the good behind their maladies. Common sense tells us that in this life we do evil to ourselves and to others; moreover, there are tragedies that defy explanation except as the tragic intersections of accidental forces. Earthquakes occur and fire burns, and people happen to be in the way and perish. Cancer pursues its dumb persistent growth without regard to its human hosts. God knows that we could all do with being more philosophical about life's reverses but not so far as to pretend that evil is good in disguise and God's will for us. No: God is no pretender and no sadist.

The Silence of Lazarus

As a young journalist, I was trained to approach every story with the standard questions: who? what? when? where? why? how? Later, as an editor and editorial writer, I added the question "So what?" The gospels, although written in a surprisingly contemporary journalistic style, are maddeningly silent about the usual queries and, if presented by a reporter to his editor, would drive the latter to distraction. To our knowledge, Jesus left nothing written except some figures in the sand, so we have only the evangelists, who offer up some geography, plot, cast, and dialogue but neglect to tell us Jesus' age, appearance, habits, and preferences, plus the other details that would make for a well-rounded natural (let alone *super*natural) account.

To my mind, the most intriguing nonstory in the gospels has to be the silence of Lazarus. Lazarus, you will recall, is the only person on record to reduce Jesus to tears. The gospel in its simple direct way relates that Jesus wept because he loved Lazarus and arrived too late in Bethany to prevent his friend's death. Lazarus had been in his tomb, wrapped like a mummy but surely decomposing when Jesus brought him back to life. Lazarus's was no near-death or out-of-body experience. He was dead as a doornail and buried for four days, then was brought back to life. What tale did he then tell of the afterlife? Was he disappointed to be dragged back? How did this world now strike someone who had tasted the next? The evangelists tell us *nothing*.

Is this some perversity on their part, or sheer ignorance of what Lazarus had to say? I am inclined to believe neither. The evangelist reporters believed that anything Lazarus might relate was only a footnote to the *real* story, which was that Jesus had proved he had power over life and death. (On the other hand, if I could have gotten an exclusive from Lazarus, I fancy that I might have been a candidate for a Pulitzer.)

We do know from the gospel reporters that Jesus himself soon followed Lazarus in death and that he rose on the third day and appeared to his friends—somehow the same, yet somehow different from the man they all remembered. Jesus, of course, unlike Lazarus, already knew something about eternity. But again, he did not regale his friends with stories about life on the "other side," and for all we know they did not bother to inquire about it. The poet Edwin Arlington Robinson presents a perplexed Lazarus, uncertain why he has been brought from death to life:

> I cannot tell you what the Master saw
> This morning in my eyes. I do not know.
> I cannot yet say how far I have gone,
> Or why it is that I am here again,
> Or where the old road leads. I do not know.
> I know that when I did come back, I saw
> His eyes again among the trees and faces—
> Only his eyes; and they looked into mine—
> Long into mine—long, long, as if he knew.

I can only surmise that this apparent lack of interest in details of the hereafter is due to the fact that heaven is not a place at all and the afterlife is not some heavenly travelogue. Eternity is neither more nor less than the intimate presence of God, which is what Jesus had been telling people all along. For the evangelists there were no adventure books to write or videos of the afterlife to show as if they were spiritual travel agents. They knew that there is nothing in our future but God.

So, as we pray for an eternity that fulfils every yearning of our hearts and fills every emptiness in our lives, we are only asking God for his company forever. May he grant our prayer.

9

Recipes from Prayerful People

"But if you don't pray, don't come!"

Eugene Rivers*

Here are some real-life voices raised in prayer. With one exception they belong to living persons, most of them Americans. Initially I was hesitant to include clergy, because (as a layperson myself) I suspected the counsel of professionals would strike the reader as mannered and technical, discouraging those of us who must make our way daily in the world. But to my surprise I discovered that the clergy's personal prayers more often than not cut close to the bone and proved to be both poignant and practical.

The following persons, lay and professional, Christians and Jews, are in no sense representative of all the people who pray. But they are sincere, thoughtful, and articulate in communicating their personal predicaments to God with love, and their example may serve you as a welcome antidote for the facile counsel I have been serving up in these chapters. The world's great chefs labor in the certain knowledge that their recipes

---

* Reverend Rivers leads the Pentecostal Azuza Christian Community in a vicious ghetto Boston police call Beirut West. When he recruits recent black graduates of Harvard and MIT to return to the ghetto to redeem it, this is his warning to them. (Quoted by Harvey Cox in *Fire From Heaven* (Addison-Wesley, 1995.)

are protected neither by patent nor copyright, but can be duplicated by anyone willing to assemble the ingredients and follow instructions. However, I have never met a good cook who didn't alter most recipes, often improving the product by personalizing it. So too with prayer. The following recipes for prayer now belong to you to make your own.

In God's Praise

I often think about the fragile poplar trees I planted around our home for security and privacy when it was new. Poplars grow tall quickly but with soft pulp and shallow roots. Over the years whole trees, grown taller than our three-storey house, cracked and fell in high winds. No longer protection but hazards themselves, they had to be removed.

Judaism is the foundation and root of Christianity. The upstart faith's roots in Judaism run deep and strong, supporting the New Covenant forged by Christ. As Jesus remarked about faith built like a house on shifting sands, it needs a surer foundation. Among contemporary Jewish writers none surpasses Rabbi **Harold Kushner,** the roots of whose faith run deep.

In his book *Who Needs God?* (Summit Books, 1989), Kushner notes that the first five minutes of the Jewish daily service are appropriately devoted to gratitude for simple things—a functioning body and mind, clothes to wear, and a day to look forward to. "Without these prescribed blessings," he confesses, "it might not occur to me to be grateful for all those things." Kushner is careful not to wait for tragedy or to base gratitude on comparisons with others less fortunate than he ("then my gratitude would be mixed with a large dose of pity"). Dispelling any notion that God is Santa Claus, Kushner affirms that prayer is "not an inventory of what we lack but a series of reminders of what we have, and what we might so easily take for granted."

The rabbi finds himself most in need of personal prayer as he welcomes needy people to his study. He prays that he will be worthy of their expectations and the confidence they place in him. He prays for the patience to listen without prejudging. "I think," he says, "that when we reach the borders of our own strength and cunning, God will take us by the hand and lead us, unafraid, into new and uncharted territory." In his prayer, Kushner seeks God's presence, confident that once we have tasted him, envy will come to an end. Gratitude will take the place of dissatisfaction, and our prayer will be that of Psalm 73: "As for me, nearness to God is my good."

From early adulthood I have admired the writing of **Herman Wouk,** who has chronicled the twentieth-century in novels from *The Caine Mutiny* through *War and Remembrance* and *The Winds of War*. Grandson of Mendel Leib Levine, rabbi of Minsk, New York, and Tel Aviv, Wouk follows the Orthodox Jewish faith, which he described brilliantly in *This Is My God* (Simon & Schuster, revised edition, 1973). Like Rabbi Kushner, he centers his prayer on gratitude for God's blessings. In a free translation of the Eighteen Benedictions of the daily service, he praises the God "who bestows goodness and owns all things . . . king, helper, savior, shield! . . . You support life with kindness . . . You raise the fallen, heal the sick, free the prisoned, and keep faith with those that sleep in the dust."

The daily benedictions thank God for knowledge, healing, forgiveness, freedom, necessities, protection, and salvation, and "for your miracles which are with us each day." They conclude with a request that is actually praise: "Grant peace, good blessing, grace, kindness and mercy to us . . . for in the light of your face you gave us, Lord our God, the law of life, and the love of good, and righteousness, and blessing, and mercy, and life, and peace."

Prayer Under Pressure

Malcolm Boyd shocked the complacency of Christians with his book *Are You Running With Me, Jesus?* (Holt, Rinehart & Winston, 1965), a compilation of prayers that destroyed the conventional distinction between prayer and real life. Confronting urban violence, racial unrest, Vietnam, and changing lifestyles in the sixties, the Episcopal priest took prayer out of the cloister and into the streets, jails, and nightclubs.

"Prayer," Boyd acknowledges, "used to stand as something separate from other parts of life," but he learned to depend less on words than on simply sharing God's presence. "My life is a life in *his*, not at all by any goodness or merits on my part but because of his love. Thus I am able to live in a kind of Christian nonchalance . . . I feel free to be completely myself with him." Boyd affirms that prayer bridges the gulf between the sacred and secular, the holy and the profane. God is everywhere accessible, "loving, in a terribly unsentimental and profound way." For those who reach out to God prayer must be not an escape from the present but an immersion in it, "however unattractive, jarring, or even socially outcast they might be."

Prayer for Boyd is not his initiative but a response to God's initiative: "I believe that Jesus Christ prays *in* me as well as *for* me. But my response is sporadic, moody, now despairing, now joyful, corrupted by my self-love and desire to manipulate Christ's love." He insists that our prayers spring from the indigenous soil of our own personal confrontation with the Spirit of God in our lives.

Michel Quoist, author of *Prayers* (Sheed & Ward, 1963), is a French Catholic priest much beloved for the simple sincerity of his prayers. Less gritty than Malcolm Boyd's, they nevertheless spring from real life, transformed by faith and hope. Quoist affirms that God takes the initiative in prayer but that "very soon the Christian must do more than imagine what God is saying to him; he must listen to him actually speaking in his life and in the world." We must quietly talk over our lives with the Father as a child returning from a journey would speak to his human parents.

Learning how to listen is the hard part: God "speaks in his Gospels. He also speaks through life—that new gospel to which we ourselves add a page each day." Affirming that nothing is less than thoroughly sacred in life, Quoist strives to see the world with Christ's eyes. "Everyday life," he insists, "is the raw material of prayer."

Prayers of Reconciliation

Vienna Cobb Anderson is pastor of Saint Margaret's Episcopal Church on Washington's frenetic Connecticut Avenue, hard by Embassy Row and just down the block from the massive Washington Hilton, where President Reagan was shot. A widow whose children died in infancy, Anderson came to ministry late and has dedicated it to celebrating the personal sorrows, joys, and resurrections of countless believers and skeptics. In her *Prayers of Our Hearts in Words and Action* (Crossroad, 1991), she confesses her weariness with

> waiting a lifetime for the Church to include the longings of our hearts in words that are inclusive and in liturgies that . . . name our dreams, struggles or sorrows [and] offer us the consolation of feeling named or affirmed as full members of the Body of Christ.
>
> Some individuals have left the community of the Church; they think they have lost their faith since the language of worship seems so foreign to the longing, doubts and fears of their hearts. Others wouldn't dream of entering through the door, assuming that whatever happens inside is archaic and irrelevant to their own life experiences . . . We have made the language of worship so abstract that it is nearly impossible to sense the joy and blessing of life in an earthy and real way. We neither laugh nor weep in Church, and that is a great pity that robs us of a deeper compassion for others and diminishes our own living.

William P. Mahedy was a chaplain in Vietnam and continued after the war to work with veterans, helping them deal with their lingering nightmares. In prayer he seeks to foster reconciliation and learn a compassion that heals. In his book *Out of the Night, The Spiritual Journey of Vietnam Vets* (Ballantine, 1986), Mahedy thanks God for deliverance from the scourge of war and prays that "we who have been scarred by war [may] be reconciled to each other, to our enemies, and to you. May we become peacemakers in all that we do."

Mahedy confesses that "we have sinned against you, refusing to love, committing the sin of Cain. But you have loved us . . . In the fullness of time, you sent your only Son . . . to open for us the way of freedom and peace."

Everyday Prayer

Kenneth Swanson served on the staff of Saint Bartholomew's, a massive church that is nevertheless dwarfed by its neighboring skyscrapers on New York's Park Avenue. In *Uncommon Prayer* (Ballantine, 1987), he relates how he begins each day at six not on his knees but in a comfortable chair, reading a chapter from both the Old and New Testaments. After reflection on the text, "I center . . . letting myself flow with the prayer until I feel deeply drawn into God's presence." He praises God, then thanks him for the joys in his life: faith, love, family, friendship, work, and home. "If I'm going through any difficulty," he confides, "I try to give God thanks for it, thanking him in advance for his wisdom and strength to enable me to grow through it."

Next Swanson turns to repentance, confessing his sins of anger, envy, greed, gluttony, sloth, and pride, asking the Spirit to reveal his hidden sins of commission and omission, seeking the strength to forgive those who have hurt him. He offers himself to God: his emotions, will, imagination, relationships, and his work. "With each category," he says, "I will be still before the Lord, asking the Spirit to show me what I'm holding back from him."

Swanson is careful not to be heroic in his requests. At one point in his life he prayed for humility after being warned by his confessor that God might answer his prayer by humiliating him. Sure enough, Swanson relates, "over the next several months I went through a whole series of painful humiliations."

Prayer in Captivity

Terry Anderson, former Beirut bureau chief of the Associated Press, suffered seven years as a hostage, chained and beaten. In the midst of his captivity my organization, the National Press Foundation, honored him in absentia. My wife and I had the privilege of spending an evening in Washington with Terry's sister, Peggy Say, and her husband. Peggy spearheaded a movement, No Greater Love, to seek by prayer and diplomacy the release of all hostages. Although her brother had begun his ordeal a lapsed Christian, he relied on prayer and regained his faith.

In his book *Den of Lions: Memoirs of Seven Years* (Crown, 1993), Anderson confirms that his capture and ill treatment could not be blamed on God: "This is not my punishment for adultery, or indifference, or all the petty dishonesties I've been guilty of in my life." A quick-tempered man, he felt justified in being angry and frustrated, but admitted "there is almost a relief in knowing that I can't do anything about these things, in finally accepting that nothing will be changed by any of this—guilt or shame or rage or frustration." The combative journalist learned to surrender himself to God, praying, "Whatever you want will inevitably be. I have no choice but to accept, do the best I can with these circumstances, with what I am."

Anderson learned in his ordeal to be grateful for past blessings, praying in sorrow for "the hurt I've given others who did not deserve it. I can't ask [God] for more, having used so poorly what he's given me . . . Instead I pray for patience, acceptance and strength for myself."

• • •

"God, give me a break, please!" prayed **Terry Waite** in captivity. As emissary of the archbishop of Canterbury, Waite, a layman, had successfully negotiated the release of hostages in the Middle East, only to be kidnapped and imprisoned himself. For 1,763 days he was chained, abused, often ill, mostly alone, with only God to talk to. He recalled his anguished prayers in his book *Taken on Trust* (Harcourt Brace, 1993).

Every morning Waite woke early to pray, but not for favors. As simply as he could, he attempted to enter into "the mystery that is God." Anglican from birth, he had long since committed the Communion service to memory and found it consoling to repeat the words and to petition for his family and friends.

Captivity was disorienting. A large, mature man, Waite found himself reverting to the confusion of childhood and the compulsiveness of adolescence. Introspection was as painful as solitude, for he discovered so much about himself that was not admirable. "I am a very ordinary man," he confessed, "chained to a wall and attempting to struggle through another day of boredom and uncertainty."

At times, try as he might, Waite did not sense God's presence and complained of abandonment. "What the hell is prayer? Nothing more than a way of attempting to soothe myself by believing everything is fine." Drowning in loneliness, his head throbbing with pain, he challenged his creator: "How dare you tell me to pray?" Yet he did, in certain knowledge that his prayers were "puny . . . but once or twice I have touched the awesome mystery which lies at the heart of the universe, and which I call God."

David Jacobsen was director of the American University of Beirut Medical Center when he was kidnapped and joined with the other hostages. In *Hostage, My Nightmare in Beirut* (Donald I. Fine, 1991), he described his seventeen months in captivity. Those hostages like Jacobsen who were locked in common cells worshipped spontaneously as a group, but each man also prayed in his solitary misery. "There were two things the kidnappers could never take away," he affirmed—"my freedom to think and my power to pray." Like his fellow hostages, Jacobsen found himself praying more for others than for himself and recalling with gratitude the blessings of his life prior to captivity. During the long months he was especially consoled by repeating two prayers he had committed to memory—the prayer of Saint Francis of Assisi ("Lord, make me an instrument of thy peace; where there is hatred, let me sow love . . . ") and the Twenty-seventh Psalm ("The Lord is my light and my salvation; whom shall I fear?").

Prayers of Faithfulness

Unlike the previous three men, **Dietrich Bonhoeffer** did not survive his captivity. Incarcerated by the Nazis in April 1943 for his support of the German Resistance, the young theologian was hanged two years later, less than a month before the war's end and immediately after conducting a worship service for the prison community. Contained in his posthumous *Letters and Papers from Prison,* the pastor's "Prayers for Fellow Prisoners" celebrated a Christmas Day in captivity with expressions of faith, hope, and love.

Bonhoeffer asked of God the grace to think only of him, acknowledging that he must have God as his partner in prayer. He thanked his creator for filling his darkness with light and for meeting his solitude and weakheartedness with companionship. With gratitude for God's gift of peace and patience in place of restlessness and bitterness, he concluded, "Thy ways are past understanding, but thou knowest the way for me."

In his prayer, Bonhoeffer praised God for his faithfulness, thanking him for the peace of the night and the light of day, then asked for strength in tribulation, affirming that "Thou wilt not lay on me more than I can bear." Addressing Jesus, Bonhoeffer remarked on the similarity of their plights, "Thou wast poor and in misery, a captive and forsaken as I am," exclaiming in hope, "Thou abidest with me when all others have deserted me."

John Dear is a young Jesuit, the son of a close friend. He wrote the following lines from a North Carolina jail while awaiting sentencing for demonstrating with others against the expansion of U.S. arms sales abroad. Father Dear was allowed a two-inch pencil stub, with which he wrote about his prayer in solitude:

"Mute prayer is my greatest weapon," Mohandas Gandhi once wrote. I very much want to be a person of prayer, a contemplative, a person who seeks God, who longs to see God face to face. But actually praying regularly and taking a prayerful approach to life is very difficult for me. It means letting go and coming before God as I really am, with all my flaws and infidelities.

Prayer is a struggle, like faith itself. I would prefer to go off to a quiet mountain place of solitude to pray like Jesus . . . but my day-to-day effort to pray more often than not comes down to the basic plea: "Lord, I believe; help my unbelief." As a Jesuit priest and peace activist who works with the homeless, I need to pray daily just to live, to love, to stay sane, to serve others, to remain faithful.

Jesus taught his disciples, "When you pray, go to your inner room, close the door, and pray to your God in secret." In my prayer I try to close the door of my inner room, to sit in silence, to let my heart and soul beat peace, to remain in God's love, and then to listen. This is my intention. It has taken me 10 years to come to this point in my spiritual life. For years I spent my prayer time venting, ranting, complaining, arguing with God about the world and telling God what he should be doing to improve it. But slowly, over time, I've come to realize that this is not how we speak to someone we love very much. In a true, loving relationship each side takes turns speaking and listening. Sometimes both just sit together in silence, enjoying each other's presence and love. Nowadays, I want to listen to what God has to say, to know how God feels these days, to be a friend that God can talk to. Prayer is a door to intimacy with God.

My prayer is simple, childlike and slow. Not much happens. My central image of God is Jesus, and so I imagine sitting with Jesus, who shares his love and peace with me and speaks to me what's in his heart and on his mind. These days, and for a long time, the risen Christ tells me, "I love you. I am with you. I want to share my peace, my joy, my love with you." Such words sustain me. After hearing them, I feel sent to share the same Spirit with others, to extend God's reign of peace, justice and nonviolent love. As Christ touches me in my poverty, I want to touch others in their poverty. As Christ disarms my heart, I want to disarm others and to be a disarming presence in our violent world, to share Christ's way of nonviolence with all humanity.

Here in jail, sitting with Christ, dwelling in the Spirit, contemplating the God of peace, I feel blessed.

10

Ten Keys to Effective Prayer

"Every day I thank God. I don't know if he has a large beard. I don't know who he is. But I thank him that I am alive each day. He doesn't owe me anything."

Brigitte Bardot, on turning sixty

There is a nearly irresistible temptation to pretend that we are praying when we are really only talking to ourselves. Letting God listen in on our thoughts and emotions is, in itself, not a bad thing, but it is not prayer. If my wife had to listen to every idle thought or complaint that runs through my mind during the course of a day, I would soon be single again. The human mind is filled with chaos—a babble of incoherence and unfiltered detritus, much of which is not of more than passing interest even to ourselves, let alone to anyone else. Psychoanalysts may achieve something through free association, but they are *paid* to listen to their patients' ramblings. God is not paid to listen to ours.

Prayer is focused attention on God. It need not be formal, but it should not be casual. As a young writer I was paid for articles and reviews by the word, but not for all the words that tumbled from my typewriter—only the good ones. Long drafts became much shorter once an editor put a price tag on each word. Later, as a journalist and editor myself, I quickly learned that a story, no matter how "big," has to be compressed into available space, and almost invariably is better for the effort. In my brief career as a preacher I was forced by my betters into the discipline of delivering a message effectively in five minutes, rather than rambling for twenty or more.

Prayer is quality time with God. Expect it to be a one-sided conversation, like writing a love letter or being a suitor. Although God is never bored and never has better things to do than care for us, he cannot be expected to bother with our blather. A protégé of former HEW secretary John Gardner tells the story of another aide who delivered to his chief a vague, rambling, and unprepared oral report. When he finally concluded, Gardner replied, "Thank you. Now you have exactly five minutes to make sense!"

Herewith some prescriptions for prayer that make sense.

1. Resist bothering God when you are only bored with yourself.

It is presumptuous to pretend that God is just waiting to convince me of how interesting and special I really am. Prayer is not an activity for times when we have nothing better to do. Prayer is the better thing to do. And here is the right attitude, expressed in the oral tradition of a hill tribe in North Bengal:

> If I ask Him for a gift, he will give it to me, then I shall have to go away. But I don't want to go away. Give me no gift—give me Thyself. I want to be with Thee, My Beloved.

2. Beware of employing prayer for wish fulfillment.

Prayer is not magic. Although God surely listens, he is more keenly aware of our situation than we are, and we might be shocked to know what our real needs are from his point of view. It is worth thanking God when your car starts in cold

weather, but don't expect God to get it started for you when
your battery is weak and you've neglected to get a tune-up. This
Chinese Buddhist prayer offers perspective:

> Have mercy on me, O Beneficent One.
> I was angered for I had no shoes:
> Then I met a man who had no feet.

3. Make friends with God through prayer.

This is the whole point of the enterprise. God has already
made us in his likeness. He loves us, forgives us, and watches
over us. We do not have to win him over. Nor is God a re-
specter of persons. He does not favor celebrities, smarties, or
sophisticates. No matter who we are or what we have done, he
remains faithful. Humble prayer rests on the realization that
God loves the sinner as much as he loves the righteous; that he
favors the homeless, the criminal, and my enemy as much as
me. The only way I can put God off is by my indifference or enmity. His friendship is not in doubt; ours is. The point of
prayer is to make friends with God. As Coleridge wrote in
"The Ancient Mariner,"

> He prayest best who lovest best.
> All things both great and small;
> For the dear God who loveth us,
> He made and loveth all.

4. Listen to God as you pray.

Prayer is not an adventure in God seeking. We don't *find* God
through prayer. God has already found you and me. Just because God doesn't carry on a personal chat with us when we
deign to offer him our attention, it does not mean that he is

not communicating with us. Much too much is made of God's supposed "silence." The Bible is nothing but the record of God's endless initiatives and messages. It would be pretentious to expect God to have some very special message for me that is different from what he has said all along to you and to everyone else from the beginning of time. We do not have to wait until heaven to know God well as a friend, but prayer without study consists of empty words and gestures. Effective prayer is the product of discipline and knowledge. John LeCarré in *Our Game* (Knopf, 1994) describes the mournful prayer of a group of Islamic freedom fighters:

> After they had prayed they made the washing gesture that I was by now familiar with, as if rubbing the prayer into their faces and at the same time cleansing them in preparation for the next one.

5. Do not hold God responsible for adversity.

In the nineteenth century, Darwin's theory of evolution upset some religious people because it replaced the pious assumption that God is constantly manipulating every detail of his creation. Nonsense, said the Reverend Charles Kingsley. All that natural selection proves is that God is not obsessed with meddling and tinkering with the universe like some machine operator. God is free to be God—to lift us up to him. As Mohammed acknowledged,

> Lord, you do not put a greater burden on a soul than it can bear. You are not angry with us when we make mistakes, but are quick to forgive us and set us right. You do not lead us into moral and spiritual danger without protecting and guiding us, so our souls can emerge unscathed . . . Lord, we listen to you, and we obey you.

Although we pray legitimately for God's protection, we acknowledge that the evil that befalls us is not his fault. God's goodness does not depend upon his making everything right. Many of the world's woes—war, oppression, crime and the like—are brought upon their victims by their fellow human beings. Other evils such as addiction and suicide are wrongs people inflict on themselves. Natural tragedies—fires, earthquakes, hurricanes, floods, and famines—and afflictions such as cancer are horrific but essentially dumb accidents that claim innocent people as victims. It is the nature of fire to burn; that it burns my house is not fire's fault, nor God's. It is revealing that Jesus in his lifetime was notably sparing with miracles. He was not a tinkerer. It is not wrongheaded to ask God to interfere with the course of creation or with humankind's freedom to follow their worst instincts, but it is inappropriate to expect that, because God is good, God *must* intervene.

6. Conclude every prayer: "Not as I will, but as you will."

This is the way Jesus himself prayed. When he was asked by his closest friends how to pray, Jesus gave them the Lord's Prayer, which includes the words "Thy will be done." Even Jesus failed in his prayers to get everything he asked for—notably an eleventh-hour reprieve from torture and execution. "If it is your will," he prayed to his Father, "let this cup pass from me." Ironically, we owe our redemption to the fact that God's contrary will was that Jesus persist to the end, which he did. While life drained from him, Jesus prayed: "Into your hands I commend my spirit." That, too, is a prayer to be emulated.

During his long lifetime Dr. Norman Vincent Peale was accused of reducing faith to the "power of positive thinking," but in this waking prayer it is clear he was only seeking God's will:

Accept my gratitude, O Lord, for bringing me to the beginning of this new day. I accept it as a precious gift from

Thee. May I use it minute by minute to do Thy will. Guide me in every problem I shall face, every decision I shall make this day. Help me to treat everyone kindly and to be fair and just and thoughtful in everything today. If I should forget Thee during this day, O Lord, please do not forget me.

7. Resist the temptation to remake God in your own image.

Readers of the Old Testament are familiar with the almost obsessive concern of the prophets that the Chosen People might be tempted to replace their invisible God with the worship of visible idols. That, after all, was the prevalent practice in paganism. Christian preachers ever since have railed against idolatry, and for good reason. It is easier for us to worship power, pleasure, and money than to acknowledge our dependence on a hidden God.

Although God made us in his image, it is a constant temptation for us to remake God in our own—to "humanize" God as our buddy, copilot, or comrade. God does not have to be patronized to be accessible. He already sent his Son to show us his face and his personality, and to teach us how to pray. When the Scriptures speak of the fear of God, they do not mean that God is scary but that he deserves the respect of his creatures. Do not yield to the temptation to diminish God, shrinking him to human size. Instead, grow in him, and you will be a bigger person.

To illustrate from a different tradition, here is a Mahayana Buddhist prayer dating from the seventh century:

Supreme One, you are an obscure mystery to us. You made all things and can purify all things. You are far beyond our understanding. Even to speak to you is to enter into an unknown region. Yet your light shines on all creatures, and your wonder illumines their souls. We beg you to leave your bright celestial palace in heaven, and come to this dusty world. Reveal yourself to us. Use your power to extinguish all evil and banish all sickness. Give peace to troubled souls. Reconcile those who are enemies, turning them into friends. Show us how we should live, that we may learn to obey you in all things.

8. Use few words, but choose them carefully.

The world is full of noisy chatter. By contrast, personal prayer is a silent conversation in which very little needs to be said. "Be still and know that I am God," our Father tells us. Because he is who he is, God has already anticipated everything we have to say to him. We have no news to tell him whatsoever. It's news only to us.

The point of prayer is to focus on God, reaffirming our dependence on him and our need for forgiveness, expressing our sorrow, our gratitude, and our aspiration to learn to love. This makes for a short but rich menu requiring few words and much meditation. Prayer is neither show-and-tell nor a discourse on "What I did on my summer vacation." The less we say, the more room we give to God to answer our prayers. Lovers and friends need to say very little to communicate; a glance or a smile can suffice. Just knowing the other is present is sufficient satisfaction. The same is true when you command God's presence in prayer. Not that this is necessarily easy, as Henri Nouwen illustrates:

> Why, O Lord, is it so hard for me to keep my heart directed toward you? Why do the many things I want to do, and the many people I know, keep crowding into my mind, even during the hours that I am totally free to be with you and you alone? Why does my mind wander off in so many directions, and why does my heart desire the things that lead me astray? Are you not enough for me? . . . Take my tired

body, my confused mind, and my restless soul into your arms, and give me rest, simple quiet rest. Do I ask too much too soon? I should not worry about that. You will let me know.

9. Don't expect inspiration.

Prayer can be drudgery. Just ask cloistered contemplatives who chant the Divine Office for hours every day, beginning long before dawn. Monks and nuns devote themselves to this repetitive exercise not because they expect any gratification but because God deserves to be praised, and people need to be prayed for. Quakers who sit together in their meeting houses, silently waiting for inspiration, acknowledge that it often does not come. They are not disappointed.

Prayer is neither an investment in gratification nor an exercise in sentimentality. Even saints confess they suffer through dry spells they call "dark nights of the soul" or "spiritual deserts," when they feel utterly empty, impoverished, and abandoned. When you hit dry patches in your own prayer, chalk it up to experience. Our relationship with God is, like marriage, "for better, for worse; in sickness and in health." We pray to God; God does not pray to us. So it often seems to be a lonely exercise. But even in deafening silence God is listening.

From the personal experience of years of insomnia I can appreciate this prayer of my contemporary Richard J. Foster:

I'm wide awake and it's three A.M., Lord.
I'm unable to turn off my mind.
I keep going over and over the events of the day.
I worry about what I said and did
Reconstructing conversations and encounters in a thousand different ways.
I wish I could turn off my mind.
I need sleep but it's like the accelerator of my mind
Is racing, racing, racing.

God, why don't you let me sleep?
I guess I'm supposed to feel pious at a time like this and pray
But I don't want to pray, I want to sleep.

10. Pray for others.

The two great commandments are that we love God and that
we love our fellow men and women. You and I have to possess a
modicum of self-esteem to be able to love others, but we don't
need to be fixed on ourselves to fulfill our destinies. Personal
prayer is, by definition, a lopsided conversation between one
creature and everyone's creator. But to be effective, it should
liberate each of us from self-absorption so we can grow in concern for others. I have no explanation for how praying for others actually works (because God by nature does not change his
mind). It is sufficient that God *tells* us to pray. In my experience, believers and nonbelievers alike are gratified by the
thought that we are praying for them. Often prayer is the only
thing we can offer to help; but the more we concentrate on
others' needs in prayer, the more God strengthens us in love
and service.

George Appleton, an Anglican bishop who compiled the
massive anthology *The Oxford Book of Prayer* (which has enriched this book), senses keenly the need to pray for others:

> Lord, I am growing old. I am slower than I used to be. My
> memory is not so good. The disabilities and irritations of
> old age come upon me. I find myself telling the same old
> jokes. Loved ones and friends pass across the frontier of
> this life and the next. Lord God, I dare to ask if in prayer I
> may keep in touch with them and they with me. May your
> beloved Son, who brings love to us, take our love to them,
> for he still spans this world of creation and the world of
> full life.

To which I say: amen.

11

A Guided Treasury of Prayers

Technique aside, the sure way to learn to pray is to copy the masters. Early in their careers as composers, Beethoven and Brahms spent countless hours tediously copying Bach's notations on paper to grasp his structure. Visit an art gallery and more often than not you will see a student with her easel and oils copying an Old Master brush stroke for brush stroke, shade for shade. One of our daughters, an art school graduate, has adorned our home with some splendid forgeries of the Impressionists. We prize them as we would the originals.

Every time you and I say the Lord's Prayer we are, in effect, forgers. It is Jesus' prayer we appropriate for our own use, but of course he meant it for that purpose. We are wise to clothe our own sentiments in the words of men and women who had a better way with words (and with God). God will be flattered, and you will feel more confident. Prayer is a language in which we seek fluency. Look upon these prayers as first lessons in that language.

Great prayers, like great poems and speeches, find their places in practically every anthology. Redundancy in this instance is a virtue—a kind of warranty that these words reflect what is in every human heart. That is my excuse for including here some of the prayers contained in my earlier book, *Growing in Faith*. Much of what follows, however, is new in the sense of being added to the earlier treasury, but not new in the sense of being freshly minted. Old prayers, far from being antiques we dust off occasionally, have the power to become utterly fresh and new each time we make them our own.

The following selection is brief and personal but will get you started.

Prayers to Start and End the Day

If you are like me, you are not prepared for conversation with your fellowman (or woman) before your first cup of coffee in the morning. But God never sleeps. It is a time to dedicate your day. Here is a delightful daybreak prayer by the humorist Ogden Nash (1902–71):

> Now another day is breaking,
> Sleep was sweet and so is waking.
> Dear Lord, I promised you last night
> Never again to sulk or fight.
> Such vows are easier to keep
> When a child is sound asleep.
> Today, O Lord, for your dear sake,
> I'll try to keep them when awake.

And a greeting by the Scottish writer Robert Louis Stevenson (1850–94):

Give us to awaken with smiles; give us to labor smiling. As the sun returns in the east, so let our patience be renewed with dawn; as the sun lightens the world, so let our loving-kindness brighten this house of our habitation.

The great English writer and lexicographer Samuel Johnson (1709–84) was a man of the world, but this was his waking prayer:

Make us remember, O God, that every day is your gift, to be used according to your command.

The following prayer from the Christian liturgy is so ancient that its author cannot be traced:

O God, who has folded back the mantle of the night to clothe us in the golden glory of the day, chase from our hearts all gloomy thoughts and make us glad with the brightness of hope.

Thomas à Kempis (1380–1471) was educated by the Brothers of the Common Life, a community formed to promote a deeper commitment to Christ. That experience prompted him to write *The Imitation of Christ,* the most widely read Christian book in history. Here is his dawn prayer:

Who can tell what a day may bring forth? Cause me therefore, gracious God, to live every day as if it were to be my last, for I know not but that it may be such. Cause me to live now as I shall wish I had done when I come to die.

And here is the prayer designated for very young Jewish children:

Blessed are You, O Lord our God, King of the Universe, who removes sleep from my eyes, and slumber from my eyelids.

I thank You, O living and eternal King, for restoring my soul to me with compassion; great is Your faithfulness.

Hear, O Israel: the Lord our God, the Lord is One. Blessed be the name of his glorious kingdom for ever and ever. And you shall love the Lord your God with all your heart; and with all your soul, and with all your might.

May the words of my mouth and the meditation of my heart find favor with you, O Lord, my rock and my Redeemer.

At day's end it is time for reflection and rededication. Lately

I have been using this Jewish prayer. Although it is intended for children, I find it sophisticated enough for me:

> Blessed are You, O Lord our God, King of the Universe, who causes the bonds of sleep to fall upon my eyes, and slumber upon my eyelids.
> May it be your will, O Lord my God and God of my fathers, to let me lie down in peace, and rise up in peace.
> Blessed be the Lord by day, blessed be the Lord by night; Blessed be the Lord when we lie down; blessed be the Lord when we rise up.
> Behold, the Guardian of Israel neither slumbers nor sleeps.
> Into Your hand I entrust my spirit: You have redeemed me, O Lord God of truth.
> For Your salvation, I hope, O Lord.

The great Saint Augustine of Hippo (354–430) composed this lovely evening prayer:

> Watch, dear Lord,
> with those who wake, or watch, or weep tonight,
> and give your angels charge over those who sleep.
> Tend your sick ones, O Lord Christ,
> rest your weary ones.
> Bless your dying ones.
> Soothe your suffering ones.
> Pity your afflicted ones.
> Shield your joyous ones.
> And all for your love's sake,
> Amen.

The chronically ill Robert Louis Stevenson composed this prayer and read it to his family the night before his sudden death:

Go with each of us to rest; if any awake, temper to them the dark hours of watching; and when the day returns, return to us, our sun and comforter, and call us up with morning faces and with morning hearts, eager to labour, eager to be happy, if happiness should be our portion, and if the day be marked for sorrow, strong to endure it.

At day's end the church sings Compline, the final hour of the Divine Office. Here from *The Book of Common Prayer* is how it concludes:

> Guide us waking, O Lord, and guard us sleeping;
> That awake we may watch with Christ,
> And asleep we may rest in peace.

Here is my favorite, attributed to Cardinal John Henry Newman (1801–90), leader of the Oxford Movement:

> O Lord, support us all the day long,
> until the shadows lengthen,
> and the evening comes,
> and the fever of life is over,
> and our work is done.
> then in thy mercy, grant us a safe lodging
> and a holy rest,
> and peace at the last.
> Amen.

Blessings and Prayers for Occasions

You do not have to be a member of the clergy to call down a blessing. Meals are traditional times for prayer. Our children are all adults now, but when they visit, we all hold hands around the dinner table and repeat this grace they learned as schoolchildren:

> Thank you for the world so sweet.
> Thank you for the food we eat.
> Thank you for the birds that sing.
> Thank you, God, for everything.

Here is a grace before meals written by the great sixteenth-century English composer Thomas Tallis (c. 1505–1585):

> To God who gives our daily bread
> A thankful song we raise,
> And pray that he who sends us food
> May fill our hearts with praise.

And another attributed to the German reformer Martin Luther (1483–1546):

> Come, Lord Jesus, be our guest,
> And may our meal by you be blest. Amen.

Here is a grace not confined to meals, adapted from 2 Corinthians 13:13:

> May the grace of the Lord Jesus Christ,
> and the love of God,
> and the fellowship of the Holy Spirit,
> be with us all.

This blessing, based on Psalm 67, has been used at least since the seventh century B.C.:

The Lord bless us and keep us, the Lord make his face to shine upon us, and be gracious unto us, the Lord lift up the light of his countenance upon us and give us peace.

There are special blessings for various occasions. Here is the blessing of Scottish reformer John Knox (1513–72) for a couple being married:

The Lord sanctify and bless you,
the Lord pour the riches of his grace upon you,
that you may please him
and live together in holy love
to your lives' end.

Temple Gairdner (1873–1928) spent his working life as an
English missionary in Egypt. Here is his prayer before his own
marriage:

That I may come near to her,
draw me nearer to you than to her;
that I may know her,
make me to know you more than her;
that I may love her
with the love of a perfectly whole heart,
cause me to love you more than her and most of all.

Prayers of Praise and Celebration

We praise God for himself and his creation. Here is the memorable Psalm 8:

O Lord, our Lord,
how majestic is your name
in all the earth!
You have set your glory
above the heavens.
From the lips of children and infants
you have ordained praise
because of your enemies,
to silence the foe and the avenger.
When I consider your heavens,
the work of your fingers,
the moon and the stars,
which you have set in place,

> what is man that you are mindful of him,
> the son of man that you care for him?
> You made him a little lower than
> the heavenly beings
> and crowned him with glory and honour.
> You made him ruler over the works
> of your hands;
> you put everything under his feet:
> all flocks and herds,
> and the beasts of the field,
> the birds of the air
> and the fish of the sea,
> all that swim the paths of the seas.
> O Lord, our Lord,
> how majestic is your name
> in all the earth!

The *Te Deum* is the great Christian hymn of praise, used since the fourth century:

You are God and we praise you; you are the Lord and we ac-
    claim you;
You are the eternal Father; all creation worships you.
To you all angels, all the powers of heaven,
Cherubim and seraphim sing in endless praise,
Holy holy holy Lord, God of power and might;
Heaven and earth are full of your glory.
The glorious company of apostles praise you;
The noble fellowship of prophets praise you;
The white-robed army of martyrs praise you.
Throughout the whole world the holy church acclaims you,
Father of majesty unbounded;
Your true and only Son worthy of all worship,
And the Holy Spirit advocate and guide.
You Christ are the King of glory,
The eternal Son of the Father.

When you became man to set us free
You did not abhor the virgin's womb.
You overcame the sting of death
And opened the kingdom of heaven to all believers.
You are seated at God's right hand in glory;
We believe that you will come and be our judge.
Come then Lord and help your people,
Bought with the price of your own blood;
And bring us with your saints
To glory everlasting.

Everyone loves Saint Francis of Assisi (1181–1226). Despite his poverty and many ordeals, he maintained a lifelong optimism and simplicity exemplified in his "Canticle of the Sun":

O most high, Almighty, good Lord God, to you belong praise, glory, honor, and all blessing!

Praised be my Lord God for all his creatures, especially for our brother the sun, who brings us the day and who brings us the light; fair is he and shines with a very great splendor; O Lord, he signifies you to us!

Praised be my Lord for our sister the moon, and for the stars, which he has set clear and lovely in heaven.

Praised be my Lord for our brother the wind, and for the air and clouds, calms and all weather by which you uphold life in all creatures.

Praised be my Lord for our sister water, who is very serviceable to us and humble and precious and clean.

Praised be my Lord for our brother fire, through whom you give us light in the darkness; and he is bright and pleasant and very mighty and strong.

Praised be my Lord for our mother the earth, who sustains us and keeps us and brings forth various fruits and flowers of many colors, and grass.

Praised be my Lord for all those who pardon one another for his love's sake, and who endure weakness and tribulation;

blessed are they who shall peaceably endure, for you, O
Most High, will give them a crown.
Praised be my Lord for our sister, the death of the body, from
which no man escapes. Woe to him who dies in mortal sin!
Blessed are they who are found walking by your most holy
will, for the second death shall have no power to do them
harm.
Praise and bless the Lord, and give thanks to him and serve
him with great humility.

Not all prayers of praise are so lengthy. Here are four lines
by the blind English poet John Milton (1608–74), author of
Paradise Lost:

> Let us, with a gladsome mind
> Praise the Lord, for he is kind;
> For his mercies shall endure,
> Ever faithful, ever sure.

And the sentiments of Christina Rossetti (1830–94):

Open wide the window of our spirits, O Lord, and fill us
full of light; open wide the door of our hearts, that we may
receive and entertain you with all our powers of adoration
and love.

Emily Brontë (1818–48), author of *Wuthering Heights,* composed a poem of praise that includes these lines:

> Though Earth and moon were gone
> And suns and universes ceased to be
> And thou wert left alone
> Every Existence would exist in thee.
> There is not room for Death
> Nor atom that his might could render void
> Since thou art Being and Breath

And what thou art may never be destroyed.

In our own time, the late Martin Luther King Jr. (1929–68) offered this prayer of dedication:

And now unto him who is able to keep us from falling and lift us from the dark valley of despair to the mountains of hope, from the midnight of desperation to the daybreak of joy; to him be power and authority, for ever and ever. Amen.

Prayers of Sorrow and Repentance

Here are two prayers linked in the Christian liturgy:

Lord, I am not worthy that thou shouldst enter under my roof: but speak the word only, and my soul shall be healed.

Based on Luke 7:6–7

Lamb of God, you take away the sins of the world:
have mercy on us.
Lamb of God, you take away the sins of the world:
have mercy on us.
Lamb of God, you take away the sins of the world: grant us
peace.

The Roman Missal

I cannot read this African American spiritual without hearing the voice of the late Paul Robeson:

Were you there when they crucified my Lord?
Were you there?

O sometimes it causes me to tremble, tremble, tremble,
Were you there when they crucified my Lord?

In a different mood, the Celtic monk Tadhg Óg Ó Huiginn
(d. 1448) asked for the miracle of forgiveness in this beautiful
nature prayer:

O Son of God, do a miracle for me, and change my
heart; thy having taken flesh to redeem me was more difficult than to transform my wickedness.

It is thou who, to help me, didst go to be scourged . . .
thou, dear child of Mary, art the refined molten metal of
our forge.

It is thou who makest the sun bright, together with the
ice; it is thou who createdst the rivers and the salmon all
along the river.

That the nut-tree should be flowering, O Christ, it is a
rare craft; through the skill too comes the kernel, thou
fair ear of our wheat.

Though the children of Eve ill deserve the bird-flocks
and the salmon, it was the Immortal One on the cross
who made both salmon and birds.

It is he who makes the flower of the sloes grow through
the surface of the blackthorn, and the nut-flower on other
trees; beside this, what miracle is greater?

John Wesley (1703–91) rode an average of eight thousand
miles a year on horseback to preach the gospel to crowds in
the open air as Jesus did. Here is his plea for forgiveness:

Forgive them all, O Lord:
our sins of omission and our sins of commission;
the sins of our youth and the sins of our riper
    years;
the sins of our souls and the sins of our bodies;
our secret and our more open sins;

our sins of ignorance and surprise,
and our more deliberate and presumptuous sin;
the sins we have done to please ourselves
and the sins we have done to please others;
the sins we know and remember,
and the sins we have forgotten;
the sins we have striven to hide from others
and the sins by which we have made others
    offend;
forgive them, O Lord, forgive them all for his sake,
who died for our sins and rose for our justification,
and now stands at thy right hand to make intercession
    for us,
Jesus Christ our Lord.

Prayers of Gratitude and Love

Here is Jesus' own expression of gratitude to his Father:

Father, I thank you that you have heard me. I know that
you always hear me, but I have said this for the sake of
these people standing here so that they may believe that
you have sent me.

And here is a Gaelic prayer of devotion:

I have serenity because I know you love me.
Because you love me, nothing can steal my peace.
Because you love me, I possess every good thing.

Anselm (1033–1109) was archbishop of Canterbury. He expressed his desire for God in this prayer:

O Lord our God, grant us grace
to desire you with our whole heart,

that so desiring we may seek and find you,
and so finding you, may love you,
and loving you, may hate those sins
from which you have redeemed us.

Erasmus (c. 1469–1536) was the most prominent scholar of his time. He prayed to be emptied of self that he might be filled with the love of God:

Sever me from myself that I may be grateful to you;
may I perish to myself that I may be safe in you;
may I die to myself that I may live in you;
may I wither to myself that I may blossom in you;
may I be emptied of myself that I may abound in you;
may I be nothing to myself that I may be all to you.

Thomas More (1478–1535), the subject of the film *A Man for All Seasons,* felt trapped between loyalty to his king and to his God, and went to the scaffold proclaiming, "I am the king's good servant, but God's first." Before he was beheaded, More made this request of his executioner: "Assist me up. Coming down, I can shift for myself." Here is a prayer he wrote a week before his death:

Glorious God, give me grace to amend my life, and to have an eye to my end without begrudging death, which to those who die in you, good Lord, is the gate of a wealthy life.

And give me, good Lord, a humble, lowly, quiet, peaceable, patient, charitable, kind, tender and pitiful mind, in all my works and all my words and all my thoughts, to have a taste of your holy, blessed Spirit.

Give me, good Lord, a full faith, a firm hope, and a fervent charity, a love of you incomparably above the love of myself.

Give me, good Lord, a longing to be with you, not to

avoid the calamities of this world, nor so much to attain the joys of heaven, as simply for love of you.

And give me, good Lord, your love and favour, which my love of you, however great it might be, could not deserve were it not for your great goodness.

These things, good Lord, that I pray for, give me your grace to labour for.

Finally, here is a request for love from *The Book of Common Prayer:*

O Lord, who hast taught us that all our doings without love are nothing worth; Send thy Holy Spirit, and pour into our hearts that most excellent gift of love, the very bond of peace and of all virtues, without which whosoever liveth is counted dead before thee: Grant this for thine only Son Jesus Christ's sake.

Prayers for Faith and Confidence

The best-known prayer of confidence in God is Psalm 23:

The Lord is my shepherd: therefore can I lack nothing.
He shall feed me in a green pasture: and lead me forth beside the waters of comfort.
He shall convert my soul: and bring me forth in the paths of righteousness, for his Name's sake.
Yea, though I walk through the valley of the shadow of death, I will fear no evil: for thou art with me: thy rod and thy staff comfort me.
Thou shalt prepare a table before me against them that trouble me: thou hast anointed my head with oil, and my cup shall be full.
But thy loving-kindness and mercy shall follow me all the days of my life: and I will dwell in the house of the Lord forever.

Dietrich Bonhoeffer, whom we met before, wrote this prayer while awaiting execution in a Nazi prison:

> In me there is darkness,
> But with you there is light;
> I am lonely, but you do not leave me;
> I am feeble in heart, but with you there is help;
> I am restless, but with you there is peace.
> In me there is bitterness, but with you there is patience;
> I do not understand your ways,
> But you know the way for me . . .

Søren Kierkegaard (1813–55) remarked of his conversion that "Christ came in through locked doors." Here he prays for authentic faith:

> Teach me,
> O God,
> not to torture myself,
> not to make a martyr out of myself
> through stifling reflection,
> but rather teach me to breathe deeply in faith.

These lines by John Henry Newman are perpetuated in the memorable hymn that seeks God's guidance:

> Lead, kindly Light, amid the encircling gloom,
>   Lead Thou me on,
> The night is dark and I am far from home,
>   Lead Thou me on,
> Keep Thou my feet: I do not ask to see
> The distant scene; one step's enough for me.

Martin Luther uses the same expression as his contemporary, Erasmus, asking God to fill his emptiness:

See, Lord, an empty vessel that needs to be filled. My Lord, fill it. I am weak in the faith; strengthen me. I am cold in love, warm me and make me fervent so that my love may go out to my neighbor. I do not have a strong and firm faith; at times I doubt and am unable to trust you altogether. O Lord, help me. Strengthen my faith and trust in you. In you I have sealed all the treasures I have. I am poor; you are rich and came to be merciful to the poor. I am a sinner; you are upright. With me there is an abundance of sin; in you is the fullness of righteousness. Therefore, I will remain with you from whom I can receive, but to whom I may not give. Amen.

Prayers in Need

Psalm 42 is an ancient cry for God's help:

> As the deer pants for streams of water,
> so my soul pants for you, O God.
> My soul thirsts for God, for the living God.
> When can I go and meet with God?
> My tears have been my food day and night,
> while men say to me all day long,
> "Where is your God?"
> These things I remember
> as I pour out my soul:
> how I used to go with the multitude,
> leading the procession to the house of God.
> with shouts of joy and thanksgiving
> among the festive throng.
> why are you downcast, O my soul?
> Why so disturbed within me?
> Put your hope in God,
> for I will yet praise him,
> my Saviour and my God.

Two other psalms express confidence in the midst of trials:

> I have relied on you since the day I was born,
> and you have always been my God.
> Do not stay away from me!
> Trouble is near,
> and there is no one to help.

From Psalm 22

> The Lord is my light and my salvation;
> I will fear no one.
> The Lord protects me from all danger;
> I will never be afraid.

From Psalm 27

We are unlikely to share Jonah's predicament, but his prayer is appropriate for anyone in need:

> In my distress, O Lord, I called to you,
> and you answered me.
> From deep in the world of the dead
> I cried for help, and you heard me.
> You threw me down into the depths,
> to the very bottom of the sea,
> where the waters were all round me,
> and all your mighty waves rolled over me . . .
> The water came over me and choked me;
> the sea covered me completely,
> and seaweed was wrapped round my head.
> I went down to the very roots of the mountains,
> into the land whose gates lock shut for ever.
> but you, O Lord my God,
> brought me back from the depths alive.
> When I felt my life slipping away,

then, O Lord, I prayed to you,
and in your holy Temple you heard me.

From Jonah 2

By contrast, AIDS is a contemporary challenge that tests the
faith of its sufferers. Here is an extract from a Litany of Reconciliation written by a victim. Its author is known only to God:

Almighty God, creator of life, sustainer of every good
thing I know, my partner with me in the pain of this
earth, hear my prayer as I am in the midst of separation
and alienation from everything I know to be supportive
and healing and true.

AIDS has caused me to feel separated from you. I say,
"Why me? What did I do to deserve this?" . . . Help me to
remember that you do not punish your creation by bringing disease, but that you are Emmanuel, God with us. You
are as close to me as my next breath.

AIDS has caused a separation between the body I knew
and my body now . . . Help me to remember that I am
more than my body, and while it pains me greatly to see
what has happened to it, I am more than my body . . . I am
part of you and you me.

God of my birth and God of my death, help me know
you have been, you are, and you are to come . . . Amen.

Here are two prayers of Saint Francis of Assisi asking for
strength in tribulation:

I will rejoice at my tribulations and infirmities
and be strong in the Lord,
at all times giving thanks to God the Father
and to his only Son, our Lord Jesus Christ, and to the Holy
    Spirit
for the great grace he has given me

in deigning to assure me, his unworthy servant,
while I am still alive, that his kingdom will be mine.

Lord, look down on me in my infirmities and help me to
bear them patiently.

Saint Augustine of Hippo prayed to be "repaired":

O Lord, the house of my soul is narrow;
enlarge it, that you may enter in.
It is ruinous, O repair it!
It displeases your sight; I confess it, I know.
but who shall cleanse it, to whom shall I cry but to you?
Cleanse me from my secret faults, O Lord,
and spare your servant from strange sins.

The great American theologian Reinhold Niebuhr
(1892–1971) composed a prayer that since has been embraced
by men and women who suffer the pain of addiction. But it
stands as a prayer anyone can adopt in times of trial and uncertainty:

O God, grant us the serenity
to accept what cannot be changed,
the courage to change what can be changed,
and the wisdom to know the difference.

Prayers of Dedication and Service to Others

The prayer of Jesus on the cross is a model for dealing with our
enemies:

Father, forgive them; for they know not what they do.

Luke 23:34

George Fox (1624–91), founder of the Society of Friends (better known as Quakers), prayed for a sense of service:

O Lord, baptize our hearts into a sense of the conditions and needs of all people.

One of the best-known prayers of all time is the plea of Saint Francis of Assisi to serve all people:

Lord, make me an instrument of your peace. Where there is hatred, let me sow love; where there is injury, pardon; where there is doubt, faith; where there is despair, hope; where there is darkness, light; where there is sadness, joy.

O divine Master, grant that I may not so much seek to be consoled, as to console; to be understood, as to understand; to be loved, as to love. For it is in giving that we receive; it is in pardoning that we are pardoned; and it is in dying that we are born to eternal life.

Francis's contemporary counterpart, Mother Teresa of Calcutta, prays for dedication in our times:

Make us worthy, Lord,
To serve our fellow-men
Throughout the world who live and die
in poverty or hunger.
Give them through our hands
This day their daily bread
And by our understanding love
Give peace and joy.

Nursing was a barely respectable profession when Florence Nightingale (1820–1910) formed a corps of women to tend for the wounded in the Crimean War. Working twenty hours a day, she brought order out of chaos in field hospitals. She prayed:

Oh God, you put into my heart this great desire to devote myself to the sick and sorrowful; I offer it to you. Do with it what is for your service.

Oh my Creator, are you leading every man of us to perfection? Or is this only a metaphysical idea for which there is no evidence? Is man only a constant repetition of himself? You know that through all these twenty horrible years I have been supported by the belief (I think I must believe it still or I am sure I could not work) that I was working with you who were bringing every one of us, even our poor nurses, to perfection. O Lord, even now I am trying to snatch the management of your world from your hands. Too little have I looked for something higher and better than my own work—the work of supreme Wisdom, which uses us whether we know it or not.

South African novelist Alan Paton (1903–88) did not live to see the end of apartheid but fought all his life for reconciliation between the races. He prayed:

Give us courage, O Lord, to stand up and be counted,
to stand up for those who cannot stand up for themselves,
to stand up for ourselves when it is needful for us to
    do so.
Let us fear nothing more than we fear you.
Let us love nothing more than we love you,
for thus we shall fear nothing also.
Let us have no other God before you,
whether nation or party or state or church.
Let us seek no other peace but the peace which is yours,
and make us its instruments,
opening our eyes and our ears and our hearts,
so that we should know always what work of peace we may do
    for you.

The life of loving service does not always demand heroism,

but it is no less valuable for its domesticity. In Puritan New England, it was the custom for young girls to embroider a sampler, usually illustrating a domestic scene, and including a verse from the Bible or another pious sentiment. Here is an anonymous prayer stitched painstakingly by a small hand:

> God bless all those that I love;
> God bless all those that love me;
> God bless all those that love those that I love
> and all those that love those that love me.

The love of God and the love of his creation go hand in hand. Condemned to death for revolutionary activities, Fyodor Dostoyevsky (1821–81) had his sentence commuted to ten years' exile in Siberia. In that wilderness he developed a great love for his fellow men and women, reflected in this prayer:

> Lord, may we love all your creation, all the earth and every grain of sand in it. May we love every leaf, every ray of your light.
> May we love the animals: you have given them the rudiments of thought and joy untroubled. Let us not trouble it; let us not harass them, let us not deprive them of their happiness, let us not work against your intent.
> For we acknowledge unto you that all is like an ocean, all is flowing and blending, and that to withhold any measure of love from anything in your universe is to withhold that same measure from you.

Brief Prayers

Jesus himself affirmed the value of brief prayers. Among other virtues, they are easily memorized. Here is a sampling uninterrupted by commentary.

Lord, what wilt thou have me to do?

Acts 22:10

Father, into thy hands I commit my spirit!

Luke 23:46

Abba, Father, everything is possible for you. Take this cup from me. Yet not what I will, but what you will.

Mark 14:36

Lord, give me what you are requiring of me.

Saint Augustine

Lord, make me according to thy heart.

Brother Lawrence (1605–1691)

And now, dear God, what can I do for you?

English child

O Lord, that lends me life,
Lend me a heart replete with thankfulness.

William Shakespeare (1564–1616)

Grant us grace, Almighty Father, so to pray as to deserve to be heard.

Jane Austen (1775–1827)

Here, Lord, is my life. I place it on the altar today. Use it as you will.

Albert Schweitzer (1875–1965)

O Lord, never suffer us to think that we can stand by ourselves, and not need thee.

John Donne (1572–1631)

O Lord, let me not live to be useless!

Bishop Stratford (d. 1707)

One of my favorite prayers comes from Canon Charles S. Martin, former headmaster of Saint Alban's School, Washington, D.C. Much has been made of the faithfulness and forgiveness of dogs toward their masters. If you have a dog (as he and I do), you will sense the poignancy of this prayer:

Lord, help me to be the person my dog thinks me to be.

Now it is time you stopped reading my words and started listening to God's voice. Ultimately, listening is the essence of effective prayer; we have nothing to say to God that he does not already know. The sole point of gathering and expressing our thoughts is to concentrate our attention and open ourselves to our creator. The most effective prayer is *passive;* however, it takes active practice to achieve the awareness, devotion, and receptivity required for contemplative prayer. Do not be discouraged. In every prayer our message to God is, "*Thy* will be done." We pray to discover God's will for us. God will have his way. He will not let us down.

Prayer is not an act of desperation; it is a habit like breathing that sustains us equally in good times and bad. Unlike drawing breath, however, prayer is a habit that requires cultivation before it becomes second nature. When complacent or angry, we are tempted to dismiss God as an unnecessary encumbrance. That is what our first parents did, and it lost them paradise.

Two final notes of caution: (1) Prayer is not a cheap form of psychoanalysis. As we develop intimacy with God, we are inclined to free-associate, sharing with him every unprocessed thought and emotion. To break through God's silence we need to restrain our outpourings and to start listening. (2) If you believe God is telling you something very different from what he tells everyone else, watch out. I am reminded of the man who stands on a busy street corner in Washington wearing a sandwich board bearing his complaint—that he is being controlled by radio waves emanating from the federal government. He is clearly dotty. In prayer it is only natural to seek guidance. But do not be disappointed to find God stingy with special messages. What he has to say applies pretty equally to everyone. He has said it already many times, and his revelation is an open book for anyone to read.

When I began this book, I dedicated it "to every grown-up child who, having long since forgotten how to pray, has learned to love," then added, "as you will discover, they are one and the same thing." As you learn how to pray more effectively, the sure way to maintain perspective is to pray with and for others. I promise to pray for you, and I ask your prayers for me. With application, we may both catch a glimpse of eternity before we are ready to enter it.

Author's Note

W ITH THE EXCEPTION of the prayers themselves, I am unable to trace this book to its ultimate sources. In any case, this is not my wisdom but the wisdom of the church and the saints and scholars whose riches I have absorbed over a lifetime. I can, however, credit those whose work I consulted while writing. I am indebted to the late English Jesuit Thomas Corbishley for his commentary on the prayers of Jesus, and to the American Trappist Thomas Merton for my appreciation of mysticism in the English tradition. The incomparable C. S. Lewis was my guide through the brambles of private prayer, and the late German scholar Josef Jungmann provided a pathway through the development of liturgical prayer in the church. Journalists are always seeking reliable sources; alas, I discover that most of mine have passed from this life. I pray that they now see God face-to-face, knowing him as he knows them—and you and me.

One source who is very much alive and active is my fellow Virginian Jim Castelli, whose recent research into the prayer practices of ordinary Americans is recounted in his book *How I Pray* (Ballantine, 1994). My introduction draws heavily on the findings and testimony that he published in the Christmas 1994 edition of *USA Today Weekend*.

Quotations from the New Testament are from the translation by J. B. Phillips (London: Geoffrey Bles, 1960). The Psalms are from the King James Version. Other passages from the Old Testament are from the Revised Standard Version of the Bible, © 1952, 1971 by the Division of Christian Education of the National Council of Churches of Christ in the United States of

America. Other prayers are taken from *The Book of Common Prayer* (The Church Hymnal Corporation and the Seabury Press, 1979); *The Communion of Saints: Prayers of the Famous,* edited by Horton Davies (Eerdman, 1990); *Eerdman's Book of Famous Prayers,* compiled by Veronica Zundel (Eerdman, 1983); Prayers by James Matthews and Geddes MacGregor from *The Lion Prayer Collection,* selected and arranged by Mary Batchelor (Lion Publishing, 1992); "A Piteous Prayer to a Hidden God" from *Conversations with God: Two Centuries of Prayers by African Americans,* edited by James Melvin Washington (HarperCollins, 1994); *The HarperCollins Book of Prayers,* compiled by Robert Van de Weyer (HarperCollins, 1993); "Grace for Dieting" from *Graces,* by June Cotner (HarperSanFrancisco, 1994); *My Favorite Prayers,* by Norman Vincent Peale (HarperSanFrancisco, 1993) permission granted by Ruth Stafford Peale; *I've Got to Talk to Somebody, God,* by Marjorie Holmes (Doubleday, 1969); *Are You Running with Me, Jesus?* by Malcolm Boyd (Holt, Rinehart & Winston, 1965) permission granted by the author; *Collected Poems of Thomas Hardy* (Macmillan, 1925); *Collected Poems of Edward Arlington Robison* (Macmillan, 1937) reprinted with the permission of Simon & Schuster; *Prayers,* by Michel Quoist (Sheed & Ward, 1963); *The Poems of Sara Teasdale* (Macmillan, 1937) reprinted with the permission of Simon & Schuster; *The Oxford Book of Prayer,* edited by George Appleton (Oxford University Press, 1985); and *The Thoughts of Marcus Aurelius Antoninus,* translated by John Jackson (Oxford University Press, 1934). The poem by Emily Brontë was included in *The Professor, Tales From Angria and Emma: A Fragment,* by Charlotte Brontë (Collins, 1954). Selections from *How I Pray* © 1994 by Jim Castelli, reprinted by permission of Ballantine Books, a division of Random House, Inc. Prayer by Dag Hammarskjöld from *Markings,* translated by Leif Sjoberg & W. H. Auden © 1964 by Alfred A. Knopf Inc. and Faber & Faber Ltd., reprinted by permission of Alfred A. Knopf Inc. Selection from *The Seven Storey Mountain* by Thomas Merton © 1948 by Harcourt Brace & Co. and renewed by the Trustees of the Merton Legacy Trust, reprinted by permission of the publisher. Merton's morning prayer is taken from *A Seven Day Journey with Thomas Merton* (Servant Publications, 1992) and used by permission of Pax Christi USA. Prayers of Dietrich Bonhoeffer are taken from *Letters and Papers from Prison* revised enlarged edition © 1953, 1967, 1971 by Dietrich Bonhoeffer, translated by Reginald Fuller and reprinted with permission of Simon & Schuster and SCM Press Ltd. Marjorie Holmes's prayer from her book *I've Got to Talk to Somebody, God* © 1968, 1969 by Marjorie Holmes Mighell, and Henry J. M. Nouwen's prayer from his book *A Cry for Mercy* © 1981, are both used by permission of Doubleday, a division of Bantam Doubleday Dell Publishing Group, Inc. Prayer by Archbishop Donald Coggan used with the kind permission of Lord Coggan. Extract from *Prayers of Our Hearts in Words and Action* by Vienna Cobb Anderson (Crossroad, 1991) used by permission of the publisher. Other references and permissions are acknowledged in the text.

Grateful acknowledgment is made to the authors and publishers for the use of these prayers. Every effort has been made to contact original sources for their inclusion in this book. If notified, my publishers will be pleased to rectify any omissions in future editions. I hope the appreciative reader will be attracted to the original sources, which are invariably better than anyone's commentary on them.

A special prayer of thanks for Fred Hills, my editor at Simon & Schuster, who believed in this book and guided me through many improvements. Another for Fred's editorial colleague Burton Beals, who scrutinized every word to ensure clarity and consistency. A prayer of praise for Chuck Antony, who challenged my theology and history on every page and made the text more reliable. Finally, a prayer for my agent, Ron Goldfarb, who fought for the book's publication. Most of all I am indebted to my wife, Rebecca, who supplied the title and the spirit of the book, and chose many of the prayers. With your interests in mind, she insisted that the text be practical, not just speculative. For all the years I have known her, she has been the answer to my prayers.

DAVID YOUNT
Montclair, Virginia
October 1995

Index

Abba Macarius, 129
Abraham, 57–58, 112, 125
Acts, Book of, 208
Adam and Eve, 56–57, 124
Adonais (Shelley), 66
Adventures in Immortality (Gallup), 160
afterlife, 161
agape, 131
Alcuin, 138
Alternative Medicine and American Religious Life (Fuller), 157
anchorites, 136, 137
Anderson, Terry,   171
Anderson, Vienna Cobb, 169
Ann, Saint, 145
Anointing of the Sick, 153
Anselm, Saint, 140
    prayers of, 197–98
apostles, healing and, 152–53
Apostles' Creed, 139, 143
Apostolic Tradition (Hippolytus of Rome), 127
Appleton, George, 184
Are You Running with Me, Jesus? (Boyd), 64, 167–68
atheists, 12
Augustine, Saint, 34, 71
    prayer as viewed by, 134–35
    prayers of, 188, 204, 208
Austen, Jane, 208
Authorized Prayer Book of the United Hebrew Congregations of the Commonwealth, 25–26

Bardot, Brigitte, 176
behavior modification, 85
    drugs and, 86–87
Benedict, Saint, 137, 139
Benson, Herbert, 84
Bernard of Clairvaux, Saint, 142
Bethge, Hans, 96–97
Beth Israel Hospital (Boston), 84
Bettelheim, Bruno, 155
biofeedback, 90, 91
Blake, William, 39, 41, 46, 103
Bonhoeffer, Dietrich, 55, 173–74, 200
Book of Common Prayer, The, 42–43, 70, 145, 146, 189, 199
books of hours, 142–43
Boyd, Malcolm, 64, 168
Bradlee, Ben, 52
Brave New World (Huxley), 86
Brontâ, Emily, 194–95
Brooks, Garth, 14
Brothers of the Common Life, 144, 187
Browning, Elizabeth Barrett, 104, 105
Browning, Robert, 112
Buddhism, Buddhists, 13, 23
    prayer of, 181–82

Caesarius of Arles, 133
Cain and Abel, 57
Callahan, Sidney, 23
Call to Heal, A (DiOrio), 153
Campbell, Joan Brown, 24

Canons of Windesheim, 144
"Canticle of the Sun" (Francis of
    Assisi), 193–94
Carmichael, Amy, 125–26
Cassian, John, 136–37
Castelli, Jim, 21–22, 24, 106
celebration, prayers of, 191–97
centering prayer, 93–96
    distractions and, 95
    trusting God and, 93–94
Chagneau, François, 161
Chesterton, G. K., 27, 44
Christianity, Christians, 12, 15, 23,
    49, 71, 72, 98, 166
    attitudes toward suffering, 154
    faith as collaboration with God
        in, 42
    healing prayers of, 150–59
    humanism, public worship and,
        145
    integrity, 156–57
    intention in prayers of, 121–22
    Jesus as integration of divine and
        human in, 121
    mysticism, 96, 98, 99, 100, 101,
        102
    orders of lay, 142–43
    orthodox, and preoccupation
        with sin, 138
    personal prayer vs. communal
        worship in, 12, 73–74, 88,
        122–23, 131, 134–36
    physical attitudes of prayer in, 35
    prayer, early, 126–28, 129, 130–32
    prayer and Spirit in, 62, 123, 125
    purpose of prayer in, 26
    relationship of, to God and Je-
        sus, 32
    shifting of devotion of, 140–41
    symbol of cross in, 129, 140–41
    Trinity of, 61, 62, 123, 139
Christian Scientists, 152
circumcision, 58
Cisneros, Abbot, 143

Clement of Alexandria, 126–27
Cloud of Unknowing, The (author un-
    known), 101
Coggan, Donald, 69
Coleridge, Samuel Taylor, 178
Colossians, Book of, 95
communal worship vs. personal
        prayer, 12, 73–74, 88, 122–23,
        131, 134–36
    in early Christian tradition, 131,
        134–36
Confessions (Augustine), 135
Contact (Sagan), 48
contemplative prayer, 77–84
    autosuggestion and, 83–84
    distractions and, 78, 82–83
    focused attention in, 80–81
    letting go in, 78–79
    monks and, 144
    patience and, 81–84
    relaxation techniques for, 83
    time for, 80
    traditional postures for, 79
Corbishley, Thomas, 112, 114
1 Corinthians, Book of, 29, 96, 119
2 Corinthians, Book of, 93, 119, 159,
    190
Cousins, Norman, 155
covenants, human-God, 31, 57–58
    reciprocity in, 58
creation, Biblical story of, 53–54
Cromer, Alan, 11
cross, Christian symbol of, 129,
    140–41
Crusades, 140–41

Darwin, Charles, 179
David, King, 59, 68, 125, 134
Davis, Martha, 83
Dear, John, 174–75
Debussy, Claude, 105
Den of Lions (Anderson), 171
DiOrio, Ralph, 153–54
discipline and meditation, 88–89

Divine Office, 135–36, 183, 189
Dominic, Saint, orders of lay Christians and, 142–43
Donne, John, 208
Doors of Perception, The (Huxley), 86
Dostoyevsky, Fyodor, 207
drug culture, 86–87

Einstein, Albert, 12–13
Eliot, T. S., 74
Embraced by the Light (Eadie), 159
Episcopal Church, American, 146
Erasmus, Desiderius, 198
eternity, definition of, 164
Eucharist, 143, 144, 145
exercise, meditation and, 90–91
Exodus, Book of, 110

faith:
    captivity and, 171–75
    as collaboration with God in Christianity, 42
    prayer and, 16–17
    prayers for confidence and, 199–200
faith healers, 153–54
Findley, Charles Albert, 147
Five Songs After Poems (Ruckert), 100
forgiveness, prayers of, 17, 69–71, 117–19
Foster, Richard J., 183–84
Foucauld, Charles de, 118–19
Fox, George, 205
Francis of Assisi, Saint, 140
    orders of lay Christians and, 142–43
    prayers of, 173, 193–94, 203–4, 205
Fuller, Robert C., 157

Gairdner, Temple, 191
Galatians, Book of, 110
Gallup, George, Jr.:
    group prayer and, 136

out-of-body survey of, 160, 161, 162
Gallup poll, 12
Garden of Eden, 53, 56–57, 58, 124
Gardner, John, 177
gender, God and, 109–11
Genesis, Book of, 11–12, 53–58
    Abraham story in, 57–58, 112, 125
    account of great flood in, 57
    creation account in, 53–54, 56–57, 124
    tower of Babel story in, 124
George VI, King of England, 62
God, 36, 39, 115, 164
    approaches to, through prayer, 67
    bothering, 177
    centering and trust in, 93–94
    as communicator, 50–52
    covenants between humans and, 31, 57–58
    as creator of universe, 53–54
    dependence on, 116–17
    existence of, 16–17
    faithfulness of, 173, 178
    fatherhood of, 109–10, 120
    finding, 29, 46, 168
    gender and, 109–11
    guilt and, 36–37
    human adversity and, 179–80
    "humanizing," 181
    inner life of, 61–62
    innocent suffering and, 39–40
    kingdom of, 112, 114, 115–16
    listening to, 168–69, 175, 178–79, 210
    mediators with, 138
    mysticism and experience of, 96–102
    mystics' *via negativa* path to, 99–100
    name of, 112–13
    nature of, 12–13, 32, 55

offending, 70
passivity and attention in worship of, 74
prayer and, 13, 14, 15, 16, 17–18, 22, 24–25, 34, 38, 42, 46, 61, 77, 106, 125, 177, 182
prayers of forgiveness to, 69–71
prayers of gratitude to, 71–72
prayers of petition to, 72–73
prayers of praise to, 67–69, 191–97
private prayer vs. communal worship of, 12, 73–74, 88, 122–23, 131, 134–36
as the "real Thou," 31, 32
relationship of Christians to Jesus and, 32
relationship of Jesus with, 61
revelations of, 47, 48, 49–62, 125
role playing and, 30–31
silence of, 16, 24, 25, 31, 48, 92, 179
silent prayers and, 33
gratitude, prayers of, 71–72
Groote, Gerhard, 144
Growing in Faith (Yount), 40, 109, 122, 185
guilt, prayer and, 36–37, 138

Haas, Ernest, 105–6
Hail Mary, 141
Hammarskjöld, Dag, 37
Hardy, Thomas, 149
Harnack, Adolf, 150
Harvard University, 11, 84
Hawkins, Walter, 128
healing:
    faith, 153–54
    prayer and, 150–59
    religious, 156–57
heaven, Lord's Prayer and, 111–12
Hicks, Edward, 114
High Star, 23
Hilton, Walter, 101

Hinduism, 13, 121
Hippolytus of Rome, 127, 129
Holmes, Marjorie, 130–31
Holy Rollers, 146
Hosea, Book of, 110
Hostage, My Nightmare in Beirut (Jacobsen), 172
Huffman, Margaret Anne, 156
humanism, Christian public worship and, 145
Huxley, Aldous, 86
hypnotism, autosuggestion and, 83, 91

Ignatius Loyola, Saint, 144
Imitation of Christ (Thomas à Kempis), 144, 187
incarnation, 120
Institutes (Cassian), 136–37
integrity, Christian, 156–57
Introduction to the Devout Life (Francis de Sales), 145
Isaiah, Book of, 115
Isaac, 58

Jacobs, Harriet, 151
Jacobsen, David, 172–73
James, William, 9
    healing prayer and, 152, 153, 157
Jerusalem, 59
Jesuits, prayer and, 144
Jesus, 12, 37, 52, 54, 59, 73
    apostles of, 106, 152–53
    baptism of, 60, 61
    healing of, 150, 151, 152, 154
    integration of divine and human in, 121
    as a Jew, 60, 120
    Lazarus and, 162–64
    life of, as prayer, 120–21
    Lord's Prayer of, 12, 23, 33, 45, 65, 107–21, 180, 185
    as messiah, 59–61
    ministry of, 60–61

mystical experiences of, 100
Prayer, 84, 91, 95
praying of, 13, 14, 41–42, 106,
    180, 197, 204
praying with, 121–23, 128, 129
relationship of, with God, 61,
    125
relationship of Christians to God
    and, 32
Sermon on the Mount of, 73,
    108, 116, 134
shifting of devotion to life of,
    140–41
Jews, Judaism, 12, 13, 15, 49, 72, 98,
    120, 166
congregational worship vs. per-
    sonal prayer in, 25, 122
expectation of messiah by, 59
fatherhood of God in, 110
origin of, 58
physical attitudes of prayer in, 35
prayers of, 23, 67, 71, 121, 167,
    187, 188
Job, Book of, 59
John, Gospel of St., 112, 115, 123
John Climacus, 129
John of the Cross, Saint, 98, 101–102
Johnson, Samuel, 186–87
John the Baptist, Saint, 150
Jonah, Book of, 202–3
Judas Iscariot, 55, 56
Judeo-Christian-Islamic tradition,
    optimism of, 54
Jung, Carl, 154
Jungmann, Josef, 138

Keats, John, 66
Kierkegaard, Søren, 30, 200
King, Martin Luther, Jr., 195
1 Kings, Book of, 111
Kingsley, Charles, 179
Knox, John, 190–91
Koran, 15, 52
Kushner, Harold, 166–67

Kushner, Larry, 22–23, 71

Laughton, Charles, 53
Law, William, 102
Lawrence, Brother, 208
Lazarus, Jesus and, 162–64
LeCarré, John, 179
Letters and Papers from Prison (Bon-
    hoeffer), 173
Letter to Diognetus, 126
Levin, Jeremy, 93
Lewis, C. S., 31, 115
praying and, 33, 36, 113
vision of eternity of, 47
Lied von der Erde, Das, (Mahler), 97
life roles, 28, 29, 30–31
Linn, Dennis, 158
Linn, Matthew, 158
Litany of Reconciliation, 203
Lord's Prayer, 12, 23, 33, 45, 65,
    107–21, 139, 143, 180, 185
addressing God in, 108–11
forgiveness in, 117–19
God's name in, 112–13
heaven in, 111–12, 115–16
kingdom of God in, 112, 114,
    115–16
"one day at a time" philosophy
    of, 116–17
as part of Sermon on the
    Mount, 108, 116
purpose of, 107
rosary and repetition of, 141
temptation in, 119–20
will of God in, 115
Luke, Gospel of St., 18, 95, 104, 204,
    208
Luther, Martin, 190, 200

MacGregor, Geddes, 28
Maharishi Mahesh Yogi, 90
Mahedy, William P., prayer and, 170
Mahler, Gustav, 96–97, 100
Mark, Gospel of St., 95, 152, 208

martial arts, 90
Martin, Charles S., 209
Marty, Martin, 23–24, 106
Mary (mother of Jesus), 138, 141
matins, 131
Matthew, Gospel of St., 73, 98,
    107–8, 110
Maugham, Somerset, 99
medicine, alternative, 155
meditation:
    biofeedback as aid to, 91
    discipline and, 88–89
    Eastern disciplines of, and
        prayer, 89–90
    exercise as, 90–91
    hypnotism as aid to, 91
    transcendental, 90
Merton, Thomas, 87–88, 92, 93
messiah, Jewish expectation of, 59
Milton, John, 56, 194
mind and body, integration of, 89
Misalliance (Shaw), 63
Mohammed, 120, 179
monasteries, monastic movement:
    devotio moderna of, 144
    Divine Office as codified by,
        135–36
    in Ireland, 138
    praying in, 136–37, 139–40
More, Thomas, 198–99
Morrison, Jim, 85
Moses, 58, 59
music, prayer as, 33–34
Muslims, 12, 15, 49, 72, 98, 120
    prayers of, 71, 120, 121
"Mute Opinion" (Hardy), 149–50
mystics, mysticism, 96–103
    aim of, 97
    Christian, 96, 98, 99, 100, 101,
        102
    experience of, 98–99
    hostility of church to, 101
    in Middle Ages, 100–101

pantheism and, 97–98
and *via negativa*, 99–100

Nakasone, Ronald, 23
Nash, Ogden, 186
National Council of Churches, 24
National Press Club, 51
near-death experiences, 159, 160,
    161–62
New Age movement, 149
Newman, John Henry, 189, 200
New Testament, 15, 52, 130, 134
Niebuhr, Reinhold, 110–11, 204
Nightingale, Florence, 205
Nixon, Richard, 113
Noah, 57
Northeastern University, 11
Nouwen, Henri, 182–83

Old Testament, 15, 52, 112, 114, 130,
    181
Olivier, Laurence, 30
Origen, 127, 129
Our Game (LeCarré), 179
out-of-body experiences, 159, 160
*Out of the Night, The Spiritual Journey
    of Vietnam Vets* (Mahedy), 170
Oxford Book of Prayer, The (Appleton,
    ed.), 184

paganism, 124
pantheism, mysticism and, 97–98
Paradise Lost (Milton), 56
"Parting, The" (Bethge), 97
Pascal, Blaise, 33, 106
    mystical experience of, 99
Paton, Alan, 206–7
Paul, Saint, 13, 29, 49, 62, 93, 94, 96,
    110, 159
    prayer and, 95, 134, 146–47
    temptation and, 119
Peaceable Kingdom, The (Hicks), 114
Peace of Constantine, 131

Peale, Norman Vincent, 180–81
penance, sacrament of, 142
Perennial Philosophy, The (Huxley),
    86
personal prayer vs. communal wor-
    ship, 12, 25, 73–74, 88,
    122–23, 131, 134–36
Peter, Saint, 55, 56, 112
Peter Damian, 140–41
Peters, Gretchen, 21
2 Peter, Book of, 110
petition, prayers of, 72–73
Phillips, J. B., 106
"Piteous Prayer to a Hidden God, A"
    (Jacobs), 151
"Pity" (Teasdale), 76
pleasures, finding God in, 46
poetry, prayer and, 66
Pompey, 59
positive thinking, 153, 154, 180
praise, prayers of, 67–69, 191–97
prayer, praying:
    AIDS and, 203
    Americans and, 12, 21–24, 50
    Augustine on, 134–35
    benefits of, 14, 74–75
    Boyd and, 64, 168
    brief, 208–9
    captivity and, 171–75
    of celebration, 191–97
    centering in, 93–96
    as collaboration with God,
        24–25, 42
    communal, healing and, 158–59
    contemplative, 77–84
    as conversation with God, 22, 34,
        46, 61, 77, 125, 168–69, 175,
        177, 178–79, 182, 210
    of dedication and service, 204–7
    definition of, 21–22, 25, 176
    devotio moderna and, 144
    discipline in, 87, 88–89
    early Christian, 126–32

Eastern disciplines and, 89–90
    effective, 13–14, 15, 44, 63, 125,
        176–84, 209
    for faith and confidence,
        199–200
    finding God in, 29, 46, 168
    focusing and, 15, 45
    forgiveness and, 17, 69–71
    goals and objectives of, 37–38,
        44, 72, 77, 87, 89, 93, 182
    God's changelessness and, 39
    of gratitude, 71–72, 197–99
    guilt and, 36–37, 138
    as habit, 209
    Harold Kushner and, 166–67
    healing and, 150–59
    history of, 124–47
    honesty and, 38
    intention in Christian, 121–22
    Jesus, 84, 91, 95
    Jesus and, 13, 14, 41–42, 106, 180,
        197, 204
    language of, 65–66
    Lord's, 12, 23, 33, 45, 65, 107–21,
        139, 143, 180, 185
    love and, 197–99
    as love letter to God, 106
    Mahedy and, 170
    mealtime, 189–90
    as music, 33–34
    in need, 201–4
    for others, 43–44, 184
    of others, 33–34, 45, 65, 185
    passivity and, 46, 74, 83, 209
    personal, 12, 14, 18, 34, 64, 73,
        123, 182
    personal, communal worship of
        God vs., 12, 25, 73–74, 88,
        122–23, 131, 134–36
    of petition, 72–73
    poetry and, 66
    popular devotion and, 143
    of praise, 67–69, 191–97

preparation for, 75–77
prescriptions for, 177–84
psalms as early Christian, 132–34
Quoist and, 151–52, 168–69
reasons for, 23–26, 30, 31, 49
Reformation and, 145–46
religious traditions and, 34
responsorial, 131–32
rosary as aid to, 141
self-confidence and, 89
self-healing and, 154–56
self-knowledge and, 38–39
sin and, 17–18, 138
skeptics and, 149–64
of sorrow and repentance, 195–97
Spirit and, 62, 123
spontaneity and, 63
starting, 44–46
Swanson and, 170–71
techniques for, 85–103
treasury of, 185–209
Vienna Cobb Anderson and, 170
as wish fulfillment, 23, 177
Wouk and, 167
zero-sum world and, 37–38
prayerful state, achieving, 75–77
Prayers (Quoist), 168
*Prayers of Our Hearts in Words and
        Action* (Anderson), 169
Praying with Another for Healing
        (Linn and Linn), 158
predestination, 39, 43
Protestant mystics, 102
psalms, 67–68, 111, 125, 173, 190,
        191–92, 199–200, 201–2
    as early Christian prayer, 132–34

Quakers, 77, 146, 183, 205
Quiñonez, Cardinal, 143
Quoist, Michel, 151–52, 168–69

Ramon, Brother, 115
Razor's Edge, The (Maugham), 99

Reagan, Ronald, 27
recollection, 76–77
redemption, 120
Reformation, 145
*Relaxation and Stress Reduction Work-
        book* (Davis *et al.*), 83
Relaxation Response, The (Benson),
        84
relaxation techniques, 90–91
relics, saints and, 138, 141–42
religion, definition of, 124
Revelation, Book of, 116
Rivers, Eugene, 165
Robinson, Edwin Arlington, 163–64
Rodin, Auguste, 77
Rolle, Richard, 101
Roman Missal, 195
Romans, Book of, 13, 49
rosary, prayer and, 141
Rossetti, Christina, 32, 68, 126, 194
Ruckert, Friedrich, 100
Rule (St. Benedict), 137

sacraments, Christian, 122
Sacred Heart of Jesus, devotion to,
        145
sacrifice, animal, 71–72
Sagan, Carl, 48
saints, 183
    relics of, 138, 141–42
Sales, Francis de, 145
1 Samuel, Book of, 26
Sanders, George, 55
Satan, 56, 57
Say, Peggy, 171
Scale of Perfection, The (Hilton), 101
Schuller, Robert, 22
Schweitzer, Albert, 208
Seals, Dan, 22
Sermon on the Mount, 73, 108, 116
Seven Storey Mountain, The (Merton),
        92
Shakers, 146

Shakespeare, William, 30, 64, 208
Shaw, George Bernard, 37, 63
Shelley, Percy Bysshe, 66
Siegel, Bernie, 155
sin:
    Adam and Eve and, 56–57
    definition of, 70
    irresponsibility and, 70
    prayer and, 17–18, 138
    suicide as, 55–56
Solomon, King, 34, 59, 111
Spirit, prayer and, 62, 123
Spiritual Exercises (Ignatius Loyola),
    144
spirituals, African American, 195–96
"Stand By Me" (Findley), 147–48
Stevenson, Robert L., 123, 186,
    188–89
Stratford, Bishop, 209
Stravinsky, Igor, 67
suffering:
    Christian attitudes toward, 154
    God and, 39–40
    human nature and, 40
    indifference and, 70
Summa Theologica (Thomas
    Aquinas), 96
Swanson, Kenneth, 170–71
Symphony of Psalms (Stravinsky), 67
Synod of Tours, 138

Tadhg Óg Ó Huiginn, 196
tai chi, 89, 90
Taken on Trust (Waite), 172
Tallis, Thomas, 190
Teasdale, Sara, 76
Te Deum, 68, 192–93
Teresa, Mother, 205
Teresa of Avila, Saint, 101

Tertullian of Carthage, 127
Thinker, The (Rodin), 77
This Is My God (Wouk), 167
Thomas à Kempis, 144
    prayer of, 187
Thomas Aquinas, Saint, 96
Thoreau, Henry David, 97
transcendental meditation (TM), 90
Trinity, Christian, 61, 62, 123, 139
Trinity Church, 78
Twain, Mark, 149

Uncommon Prayer (Swanson), 170
USA Today Weekend, 21

Varieties of Religious Experience, The
    (James), 157–58
Vatican Council, Second, 141
vespers, 131
via negativa, mysticism and, 99–100

Wagner, Richard, 105
Waite, Terry, 172
Washington Post, 52
Watson, Doc, 107
Watts, Isaac, 60
Wesley, Charles, 60
Wesley, John, 102, 196–97
White House, 50
Whittier, John Greenleaf, 94
Who Needs God? (Kushner), 166
Wilde, Oscar, 37
Will to Believe, The (James), 157
Wouk, Herman, 167

Yahweh, 58, 113, 115
yoga, 89–90

zero-sum world, prayer and, 37–38

About the Author

DAVID YOUNT, D.D., is an award winning newspaper editor, editorial writer, college dean, foundation executive, and author. A member of Phi Beta Kappa, he completed graduate studies in theology at Saint Paul's College in Washington and the Institut Catholique in Paris, and was awarded an honorary doctorate by the American Biblical Institute. He was the chairman of the College of Preachers in Washington, D.C., a member of the executive committee of Washington National Cathedral, and president of the National Press Foundation in Washington, the leading organization serving the professional development of the nation's journalists. He is married with three daughters and lives on a lake in Montclair, Virginia with his wife, three aged cats, and a young Scottish terrier.